THE
ELLESMERE AND LLANGOLLEN
CANAL

THE
ELLESMERE AND
LLANGOLLEN CANAL

AN HISTORICAL BACKGROUND

by

E. A. WILSON, M.A.

PHILLIMORE

1975

Published by
PHILLIMORE & CO., LTD.,
London and Chichester
Head Office: Shopwyke Hall, Chichester,
Sussex, England

ISBN 0 85033 109 9

Text set in 11pt. Baskerville

Printed by Unwin Brothers Limited
at The Gresham Press
Old Woking, Surrey.

To my wife,
and David, Richard and Christopher,
whose help made this book possible.

CONTENTS

LIST OF PLATES
(between pages 52 and 53)

LIST OF FIGURES

PREFACE

This does not seek to be a definitive history of the Ellesmere Canal, for that has already been written by C. A.
Hadfield and L. T. C. Rolt. Instead it offers a well-illustrated
account of the canal's historical background, which may be
perused during restful moments on a canal cruise and also be
of interest to those who enjoy the study of industrial archaeo-
logy. The book, which is the result of over 20 years' research,
contains many photographs of features which, although they
could still be seen 15 or 20 years ago, have now disappeared
for ever.

The canal has had so many different names and owners
during the course of its history that some explanation of
them seems necessary in view of the fact that even its present
owners, British Waterways, seem confused as to which part is
which: they have placed a notice board at Welsh Frankton
stating, 'The Montgomeryshire Canal starts here', whereas
that canal begins at the Carreghofa locks just south of
Llanymynech!

The following table outlines the most important changes
of name and ownership:

1793   Act of Parliament obtained, and construction
        begun on *The Ellesmere Canal.*

1805   The Ellesmere Canal opened along its whole length:
        across the Wirral; along the Chester Canal, and
        again as the Ellesmere Canal from Hurleston Junc-
        tion to Pontcysyllte Aqueduct ('Water Line' not
        completed until 1808); with branches to Llany-
        mynech, Weston Lullingfields and Edstaston,
        and short arms at Ellesmere and Whitchurch.

1813   Amalgamation with Chester Canal to become the
        Ellesmere and Chester Canal.

1845   Absorbed by the Birmingham and Liverpool Canal Company.

1846   Became part of the Shropshire Union Railways and Canal Company, the canal part being referred to as *The Shropshire Union Canal (S.U.C.)*.

1846   The canal was almost immediately leased to the London and North Western Railway Company.

1917   Burst at Dandyfields on Weston branch—navigation limited to Hordley Wharf.

1922   Became part of the London, Midland and Scottish Railway Company on the re-grouping of the railways.

1936   Burst on the Llanymynech line—no commercial traffic after this on this line, or on the Welsh-Frankton-Llantisilio line.

1944   Act of Parliament for the abandonment of the Montgomeryshire Canal with its Guilsfield branch and the Llanymynech, Weston and Edstaston branches, and the Whitchurch arm of the Ellesmere Canal.

1948   The only remaining navigable part of the Ellesmere Canal—the section from Hurleston, through Ellesmere to Llantisilio—came under the ownership of the British Transport Commission.

1963   This part of the canal was taken over by the British Waterways Board and its name was changed to *The Llangollen Canal*.

CHAPTER 1

HOW IT ALL BEGAN

In Ellesmere the canal is taken for granted, and when I tried to collect information about its history I was offered little beyond boyhood reminiscences by 'the locals'. However, from the Canal Maintenance Depot I was able to borrow a report headed:

Report
to
the General Assembly of
the Ellesmere Canal Proprietors
held in the Royal Oak Inn,
Ellesmere, on the 27th.Day of November,1805
to which is annexed
the Oration
delivered
at the Pontcysyllte Aqueduct
on its first opening, November 26th.1805.
Printed by Order of the General Assembly
the Right Honourable
the Earl of Bridgewater, Chairman.

This meeting was held just after the Battle of Trafalgar. The subject of the Report was set out under five headings, and under the first it was pointed out that,

The Ellesmere Canal, rather than being one general Canal, is a system of Canals, distributed over that extensive and fertile country, which lies between the banks of the Severn on the South, and those of the River Mersey upon the North; and between the skirts of North Wales on the West, and the borders of Staffordshire on the East; a space of fifty miles in length and more than twenty in breadth. This Canal will unite the Rivers Severn, Dee and Mersey, and will open an inland navigation from the above mentioned districts to the Ports of Liverpool and Bristol. Although the commercial connexions established by means of this Canal, will be far from inconsiderable, yet it is from fuel and manure for agricultural purposes that its most important and permanent revenue must be looked for.

This needs some explanation. When the canals were first built, the English economy was still essentially rural. London had a population of about 700,000 and in the provinces only Bristol, and possibly Manchester, had over 50,000 inhabitants. Industries such as mining, iron smelting and the manufacture of pottery were trying to expand, but their efforts were hampered by poor communications. The roads were terrible, particularly during the winter, and there were, of course, no railways, so transport was not only slow but difficult and expensive. It was in an effort to overcome such difficulties that the Duke of Bridgewater employed Brindley to construct a 10 mile canal between Manchester and the Bridgewater mines at Worsley. Opened in 1761, this canal immediately halved the retail price of coal in Manchester.

The success of this and the subsequent Bridgewater Canal began a canal-building boom, which reached such a peak between 1792 and 1793 that these years are sometimes called the age of the 'canal mania'. The gullible public invested its money in any and every canal-building scheme. Many were unsound, if not fraudulent; but the Ellesmere Canal Scheme was well based and paid modest dividends to its shareholders.

It is difficult for us to picture the enthusiasm which greeted the promotion of this canal, but we may glimpse something of it - as well as of the promoters' integrity - between the pompous lines of the company's 1805 *Report*, which says,

> the paroxysm of commercial ardour of the memorable tenth of September 1792 can never be forgotten by the writer, who had the honour to be left to defend the hill near the town of Ellesmere, which gives its name to the undertaking, from the excessive intrusion of too ardent speculation; the books were opened about noon, and ere sun set near a million of money was confided to the care of the Committee. This wonderful act of public confidence was in a few days justified, by returning of all the money or value of shares not wanted for the works then projected, to those who had so liberally supplied it.

The canal's shares had a nominal value of £100. This was a lot of money for the ordinary townsman and we find that most shareholders owned under five shares, sometimes in partnership, while some held only a fraction of a share - in 1822 the Vicar of Ellesmere held 10 shares while his curate owned half one.

The whole value of the shares did not have to be paid immediately. After an initial payment, the rest of the money was paid on 'call'. In local papers of the time we find statements like 'Ellesmere Canal Navigation, 1.April.1796 - a call of 5% by May.5th.' These 'calls' were made when money was needed to pay for works in hand and of course the faster the progress the more calls had to be made. No one likes parting with money and if the demands were too frequent some holders either refused to pay or sold their shares.

The Ellesmere Canal Company had a lot of expenses to meet. As we shall see, many route surveys were undertaken and 13 private Acts of Parliament were necessary before the canal was finished. These involved much expense at Westminster. The company's solicitors claimed such sums as £3,060, £3,156, £2,836 and £1,802 for services rendered. These would include not only drawing up the Acts and arguing the company's case before Parliament, but also dealing with local disputes, with landowners, with millowners - who feared the canal would deprive them of water - with turnpike authorities - who feared loss of trade - etc.

Most of the building work was done under contract, or paid for by 'measure and valuation'. For instance, the Wirral Line involved a total expenditure of £68,405 19s. between 1793 and 1805. This included

> Weston and Fletcher: for works performed partly by contract and partly by measurement and valuation £32,679 - 5 - 5.

The surveyor, also spoken of as an engineer, on whom most reliance seems at first to have been placed was a local man from Oswestry, John Duncombe. In the financial section of the 1805 *Report* we find,

> John Duncombe, for salary in making surveys, sections, plans, attending Parliament, and acting as resident engineer to the Company from 1791 to June, 30. 1803, including all travelling and other expenses allowed him £4,402.

One of the earliest of the many variations on the original plan was the proposal which came to be known as the Eastern Canal Scheme. It was surveyed by one Joseph Turner in conjunction with Thomas Morris, John Chamberlain and William Cowley. Their plan, dated 1792, was for the canal to cross the Wirral, use the Chester Canal as far as Tattenhall, and

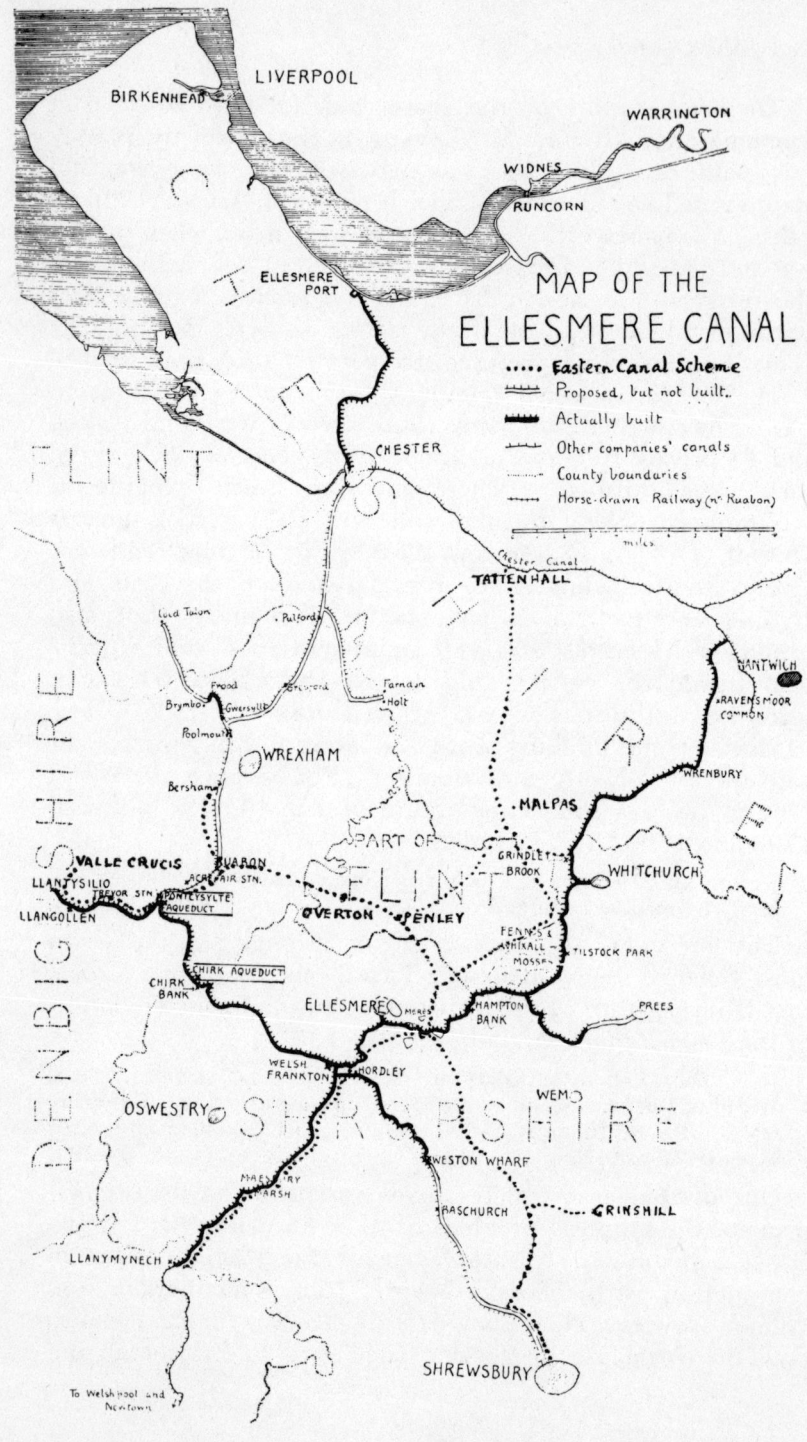

MAP OF THE
ELLESMERE CANAL

····· Eastern Canal Scheme
⌁⌁⌁ Proposed, but not built.
▬▬▬ Actually built
⎓⎓⎓ Other companies' canals
·-·-· County boundaries
┼┼┼┼ Horse-drawn Railway (nr Ruabon)

LIVERPOOL
BIRKENHEAD
WARRINGTON
WIDNES
RUNCORN
ELLESMERE PORT
CHESHIRE

FLINT
CHESTER
Chester Canal
TATTENHALL
NANTWICH
RAVENSMOOR COMMON
Pulford
Broad
Gwersyllt
Farndon
Holt
WRENBURY
WREXHAM
MALPAS
PART OF FLINT
GRINDLEY BROOK
WHITCHURCH
VALLE CRUCIS
RUABON
ACREFAIR STN.
LLANTYSILIO
TREVOR STN. PONTCYSYLTE AQUEDUCT
OVERTON PENLEY
LLANGOLLEN
FENN'S WHIXALL MOSS
TILSTOCK PARK
CHIRK AQUEDUCT
CHIRK BANK
ELLESMERE
HAMPTON BANK
PREES
MERES
DENBIGHSHIRE
WELSH FRANKTON HORDLEY
OSWESTRY SHROPSHIRE
WEM
WESTON WHARF
MAENTWROG MARSH
BASCHURCH GRINSHILL
LLANYMYNECH
To Welshpool and Newtown
SHREWSBURY
Brymbo
Poolmouth
Bersham
Coed Talon
miles

then pass southward through relatively low-lying country.
The opposed Western Canal Scheme suggested that the canal
should run southwards from Chester over higher ground
(see plans 1 and 2).

Both routes involved costly engineering problems in
bringing the canal up from the Cheshire plain to the hilly
districts where coal, iron, lead, limestone and other minerals
were waiting to be transported. Turner proposed to solve the
difficulties by means of a branch line from Penley via Overton
- five miles north of Ellesmere - to Ruabon, dividing there on
the one hand to Bersham, where Wilkinson had iron works,
and on the other, along the Vale of Llangollen to the Irenant
Slate Quarries, close to the Valle Crucis Abbey. Further
branches were proposed to Whitchurch, to the limestone
quarries at Llanymynech and the stone quarries at Grinshill.

The Western Canal Scheme was far bolder - and more
difficult. It resulted from a plan produced by John Duncombe
and subsequently modified by William Jessop, the engineer
appointed to supervise the whole Ellesmere scheme.
Considering the state of civil engineering in 1792, Jessop's
proposals were truly amazing. The canal was to climb from
the flat Cheshire plain, rise 303 ft. to Ruabon, pass through a
tunnel 4,607 yds. long and cross the two, deep, wide valleys
of the Dee and Ceiriog on aqueducts of unprecedented height
and length. There were to be two more tunnels, one nearly a
mile long at Chirk, another of a quarter of a mile at Baschurch,
followed by locks to control the fall of 150 ft. down to the
river at Shrewsbury. The plan included branches to Holt and
Llanymynech.

These astounding proposals daunted even the most
optimistic of the committee and Jessop was asked to make a
fresh survey; he decided the tunnel near Ruabon could be
avoided by taking the canal even higher! One member of the
committee said they would rather spend £5,000 on surveys
than go to Parliament with a plan based on inaccurate ones.

Early in 1793, the supporters of the Eastern and Western
schemes decided to join forces and they obtained an Act of
Parliament authorising an expenditure of £400,000, and
£100,000 more if necessary, for building the canal. Even after

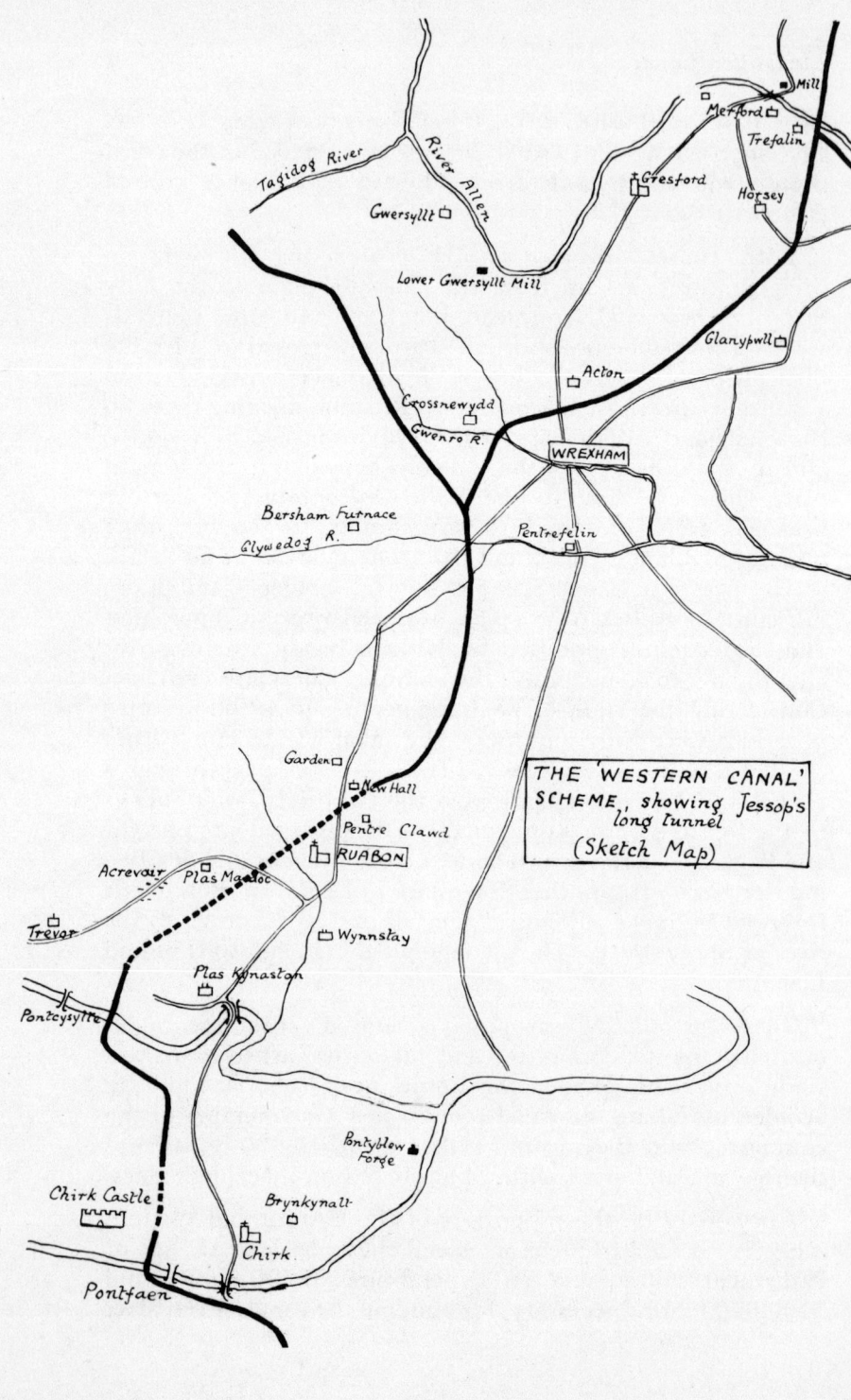

THE 'WESTERN CANAL'
SCHEME, showing Jessop's
long tunnel
(Sketch Map)

work had begun on it, many alterations were suggested to the scheme originally put before Parliament. Some of these later proposals will be discussed in Chapter 2.

In September 1793 the committee engaged yet another engineer, Thomas Telford. His duties were so multifarious that it is difficult to know exactly where they ended and whether he was regarded as a man or a miracle! Telford was appointed as general agent, surveyor, engineer, architect and overlooker, and clerk to the committee - to make reports, to superintend the cutting, forming and making of the canal, to make drawings, to give instructions for contracts, to pay the contractors, workmen and others employed, to keep accounts, produce the same, and pay the balance; to pay out such sums of money as the proprietors, committee or sub-committee should require. He was to be responsible for forming and directing the making of bridges, aqueducts, tunnels, locks, building reservoirs, wharfs and other works. He also had the duty of collecting money from shareholders as required for work in progress. For all this work he was to be paid the sum of £500 per year, from which he had to pay his own clerk and assistant, and find a surety of £5,000. After a few months Telford had his salary altered to £300, on the understanding that the Company would pay his assistants. Some time later he got rid of the duty of collecting money from shareholders.

Why so many people were required to do similar jobs is puzzling. In the financial section of the 1805 *Report* the following surveyors and map makers are given, along with the payments made to them during the construction of the canal,

John Duncombe	£4,402
Davies and Jebb	3,010
William Jessop	1,103
William Turner	763

Several others received smaller payments.

From the company's Minutes we learn that John Duncombe and William Turner were subordinate to Telford, but that Telford himself was subordinate to William Jessop. While Duncombe seems to have accepted the situation philosophically, Turner was annoyed at being supplanted. A local engineer from Whitchurch, he was a real 'stormy petrel' and his original mind and boundless energy were to cause much trouble as he criticised plans already put forward, and suggested further modifications. His insistence that his own plans were better and cheaper than others annoyed the committee, which said his surveys were so hurried and incomplete that it could not accept them. A dispassionate reappraisal of his ideas suggests that many of them were in fact sound.

Soon after Telford's appointment Turner wrote to Jessop suggesting that Telford could not act properly as an engineer while he had to devote a part of his time to collecting money. Jessop replied,

> I am quite unacquainted with Mr. Telford and his character; from the little acquaintance I have had with you I wish you might have the direction of that part of the business which you have proposed to undertake, and I do not think the terms you have offered to undertake it for are unreasonable. If the Committee should consult me on this question I should tell them so.

At the next meeting of the committee the following resolution was passed:

> It is the unanimous sense of the Committee that Mr. William Turner, the Architect to this Concern, Mr. John Duncombe their engineer, and Mr. Arthur Davies their surveyor and valuer of such lands as may be made use of for the purpose of this concern, have, by their abilities and diligent attention to the interests of the Company merited the confidence and good opinion of this Committee and of the Proprietors at large.

This attempt at pouring oil on troubled waters resulted in an uneasy partnership, with Turner feeling a sense of injury as several of his suggestions were turned down and Jessop began to work more with Telford, whose energy and efficiency he soon came to admire. Matters finally came to a head over the question of the Pontcysyllte Aqueduct, which will be discussed in Chapter 3.

CHAPTER 2

THE BUILDING OF THE CANAL

As we have seen, the Ellesmere Canal Company planned that the main line of its waterway should stretch from the Mersey to the Severn. A glance at the map on page 4 will show it never realised its ambition. For some, undetermined, reason, the southern part of the line was cut short rather less than half-way between Ellesmere and Shrewsbury. Duncombe's daring Western Scheme for the central part of the line was abandoned north of Pontcysyllte, while Turner's Eastern Scheme fell through entirely (a link was eventually made between the Ellesmere and Chester canals, but this ran much farther east than Turner had suggested). Eventually, the Ellesmere Canal comprised a line across the Wirral Peninsula and four branches radiating from Welsh Frankton, tenuously linked with the Wirral Line via the Chester Canal.

In April 1793 when the Ellesmere Canal Company's first Act of Parliament was passed, all this lay in the future. Full of enthusiasm, the Proprietors ordered building to begin at once on the nine miles of waterway from the Mersey to the Dee. This part of the canal was opened on 1 July 1795.

The Wirral Line

The line began at a small hamlet, called Netherpool, on the Mersey Estuary. It had no port, but as the canal's trade increased, so Netherpool grew, developing into the important terminus now called Ellesmere Port - the port of the Ellesmere Canal (see Chapter 4). The southern end of the line joined the River Dee at Chester.

The canal followed a level course, so locks were only needed at either end. At Ellesmere Port there were three. Here the canal widened into an upper basin, connected with

9

a lower one by two pairs of locks. The third lock led to a tidal basin communicating with the Mersey. At Chester, access to the Dee was obtained through the locks and basin of the Chester Canal.

The Ellesmere proprietors decided to build this line wide enough to carry the barges used on the Mersey and Dee estuaries. These were 14 ft. wide, double the size of the usual canal 'narrow boat', so the Wirral Line had to be twice as wide as a conventional canal. Of course this made it unusually expensive to build. Moreover, both the Mersey and the Dee are tidal rivers. The company's reports show that the tide works were also expensive, not only to build, but to maintain.

Every time a boat passed through a lock on the canal some 60,000 gallons of water were withdrawn from its highest level - known as the 'summit level' - passed to a lower one and finished up in the Mersey or Dee estuary, creating a problem of water supply. At Chester, this was met by the Chester Canal Company's agreeing to supply some water from its canal. At Ellesmere Port, a Boulton and Watt steam engine was used to pump water from the tideway into the canal; it cost £1,576 0s. 6d., and was made under licence by John Wilkinson, a famous iron founder and an influential member of the canal's committee.

The Llanymynech Branch and its Upper and Lower Line

The Montgomeryshire Canal Company obtained its Act of Parliament a year later than the Ellesmere one. The Montgomeryshire Canal was planned so that some of its water could be supplied by feeders from the River Tanat near Llanyblodwel and then would pass through Welshpool to Newtown. Like the Ellesmere Canal as a whole, it was intended to serve the farmer rather that the industrialist, and members of the Ellesmere Company hoped the two canals would be linked. As work was already under way on Ellesmere's most important Llanymynech branch - called the Lower Line - from Welsh Frankton to the Llanymynech limestone quarries, some members of the Ellesmere Committee urged that a second, roughly parallel, Upper Line be cut from near Chirk, via the Porthywaen limestone quarries to the

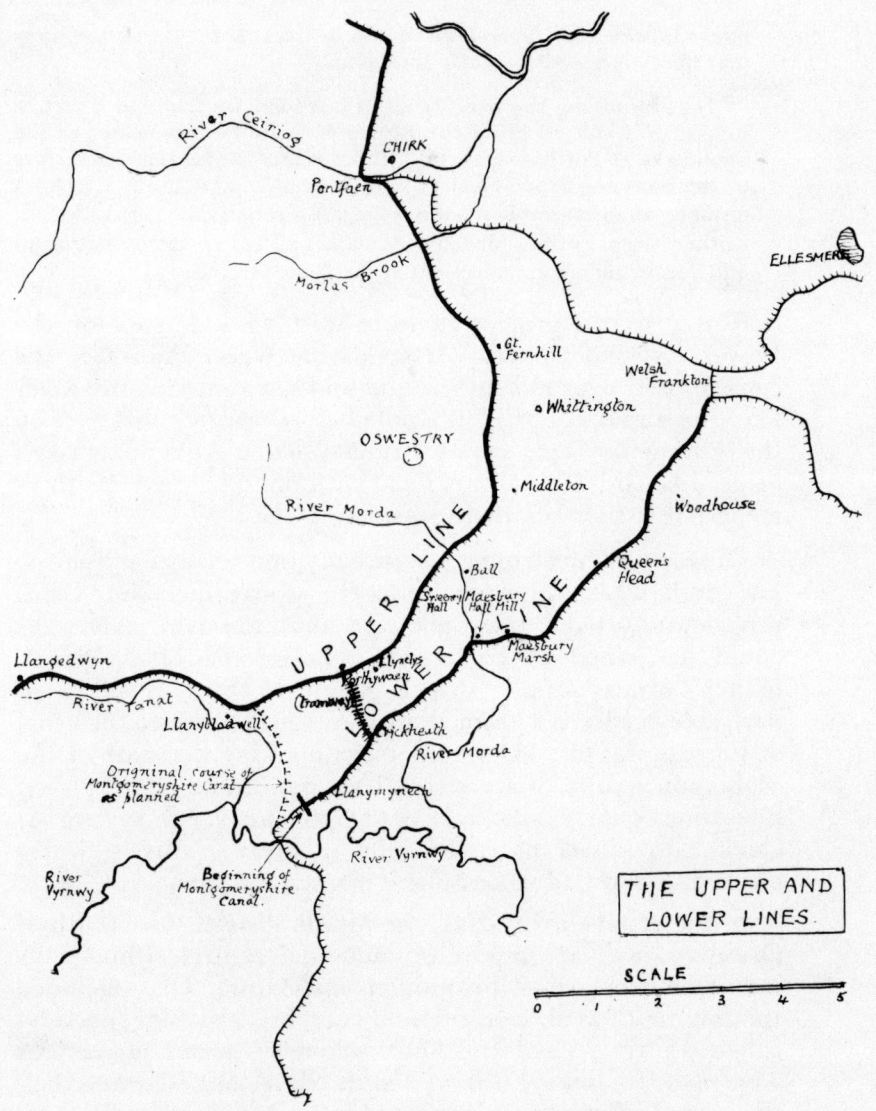

River Ceiriog

CHIRK

Pontfaen

Morlas Brook

ELLESMERE

Gt. Fernhill

Welsh Frankton

Whittington

OSWESTRY

River Morda

Middleton

Woodhouse

UPPER LINE

LOWER LINE

Ball

Sweeny Maesbury
Hall Hall Mill

Queen's
Head

Maesbury
Marsh

Llangedwyn

River Tanat

Llynclys
Porthywaen

Crickheath

River Morda

Llanyblodwell

Crickheath

Original course of
Montgomeryshire Canal
as planned

Llanymynech

River
Vyrnwy

Beginning of
Montgomeryshire
Canal.

River Vyrnwy

THE UPPER AND
LOWER LINES.

SCALE

0   1   2   3   4   5

River Tanat and Llangedwyn (see plan 3). In a manuscript
note made in October 1794 by Mr. Knight, a member of the
Ellesmere Committee, we read,

> **Reasons why the Upper Line should be executed - notwithstanding
> that the Lower Line is nearly complete.**
>
> That by taking the river Tanat as a feeder, we shall get a certain
> supply of water to bring the Rhuabon Coals 4 miles nearer to the
> limeworks at Porthywaen, and 2 miles nearer to Oswestry, and close
> to the Sweeney Stone Quarry, upon a dead level without a lock - a
> distance of about 4 miles - land to be cut through rather gravelly, but
> neither deep cutting or embankment, except a deep cutting at
> Middleton, and an embankment at the River Morda.

However, this project came to nothing and work on the
Lower Line continued. After leaving Welsh Frankton, the
canal passed over marshy ground and ran alongside the River
Perry for about a quarter of a mile before crossing this river on
the Ellesmere Canal's only Brindley Type Aqueduct, i.e. a
bridge-like, brick structure, lined with puddled clay. Its three
arches are little more than culverts.

The Llanymynech branch eventually finished at Carreghofa,
just south of Llanymynech itself. The Montgomeryshire Canal
proprietors altered their plans so that the two waterways
could be joined at Carreghofa. Later, the Llanymynech
branch's water-supply was augmented by a small, non-
navigable feeder cut from the River Tanat to meet the canal
at Carreghofa, just before the locks marking the start of the
Montgomeryshire waterway. The important Porthywaen
limestone quarry was connected to the canal system at
Crickheath Wharf by a 2½ mile tramway. This is clearly
marked on old Ordnance Survey maps.

In the canal's early days, the Morda district, just south of
Oswestry, was an important industrial centre, although its
industries were small by modern standards. They included
the mining of coal, iron ore and clay, brick making, pottery,
calico printing, wool and flour milling. Various suggestions
were made for linking this area to the canal and Sweeney Hall,
the centre of one of the largest industrial 'estates' in the area,
is often mentioned in plans. One unsigned set of 11 November
1795 shows plans for two canal branches to Sweeney Hall,

one from the main line at Great Fernhill, near Hindhead,
running via Whittington and Aston; the other from Welsh
Frankton, via Queen's Head, Fox Hall and Ball. Other
proposals for the same date include a branch from Fernhill to
Sweeney Hall passing near Whittington and Middleton to
cross the Oswestry to Queen's Head road near Milehouse and
then run via Weston Mill to Sweeney Hall and Llynclys, close
to the Porthywaen quarries. Another suggestion was for a
branch along the Tanat valley from Llynclys. For various
reasons, none of these proposals came to anything. Later, in
1800, Jessop suggested building a tramway 'towards Oswestry
and the collieries there'. The Ellesmere Company did not
follow up this suggestion either, but in 1813 a private tramway
was built by the colliery owners (see pages 69-73).

The Old Canal

A glance at the 2½ in. Ordnance Survey map, sheet 33/32,
shows an isolated ditch near Rednal, marked as 'Old Canal'.
In the 18th century the nearby house and park of Woodhouse
were part of the estates of the Rev. John Robert Lloyd, one
of the original members of the Ellesmere Canal Committee.
When the Llanymynech branch was being cut in this area,
Lloyd persuaded the committee to divert the line so that it
ran close to Woodhouse. He paid the cost of the abandoned
piece of the 'Parliamentary Line' which had already been cut.
This agreement is recorded in the company's Minutes for
27 November 1799. Later, for some unexplained reason, it
was decided to revert to the original line. The company repaid
Lloyd and he agreed to let it have enough land to widen the
canal bridle-path into the road which today runs close to the
canal as far as Queen's Head. The abandoned diversion
became less and less like a canal and today it is a mere ditch,
though still labelled 'Old Canal'.

The Frood Branch.

Old maps of North Wales, dated 1805, show, not far from
Wrexham, a completely isolated piece of canal only three
miles long. Why was it ever dug? The canal company's
Minutes do not give any definite answer. The most likely one

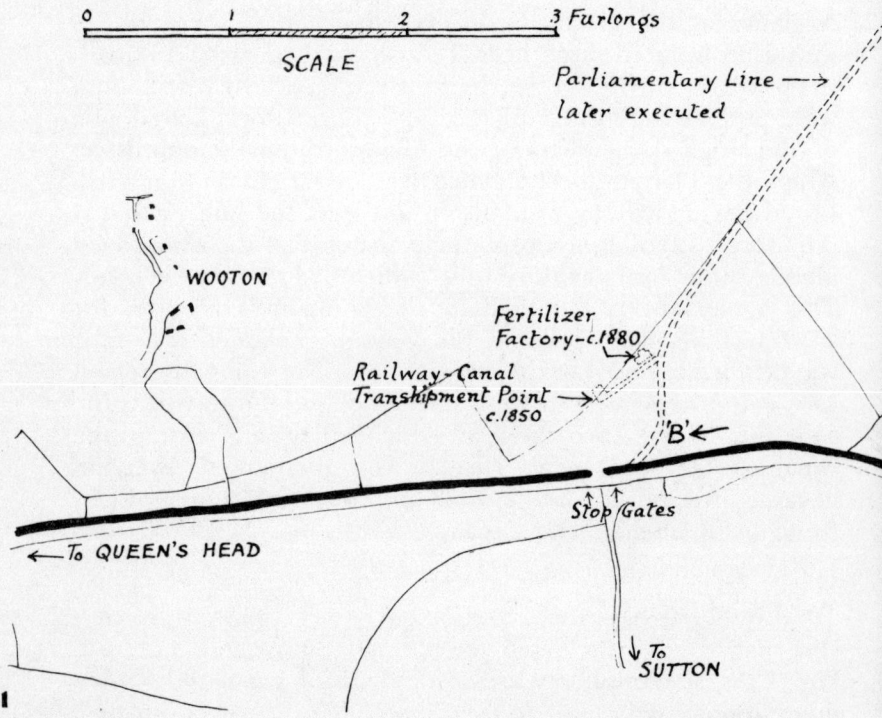

OLD MAP SHOWING TEMPORARY DIVERSION OF CANAL
TO WOODHOUSE — LATER ABANDONED AND CALLED
'OLD CANAL'

Later additions (shown dotted), described in text.

0   1   2   3 Furlongs
SCALE

Parliamentary Line ──→
later executed

WOOTON

Fertilizer
Factory-c.1880

Railway-Canal
Transhipment Point
c.1850

'B'←

← To QUEEN'S HEAD

Stop Gates

↓ To
SUTTON

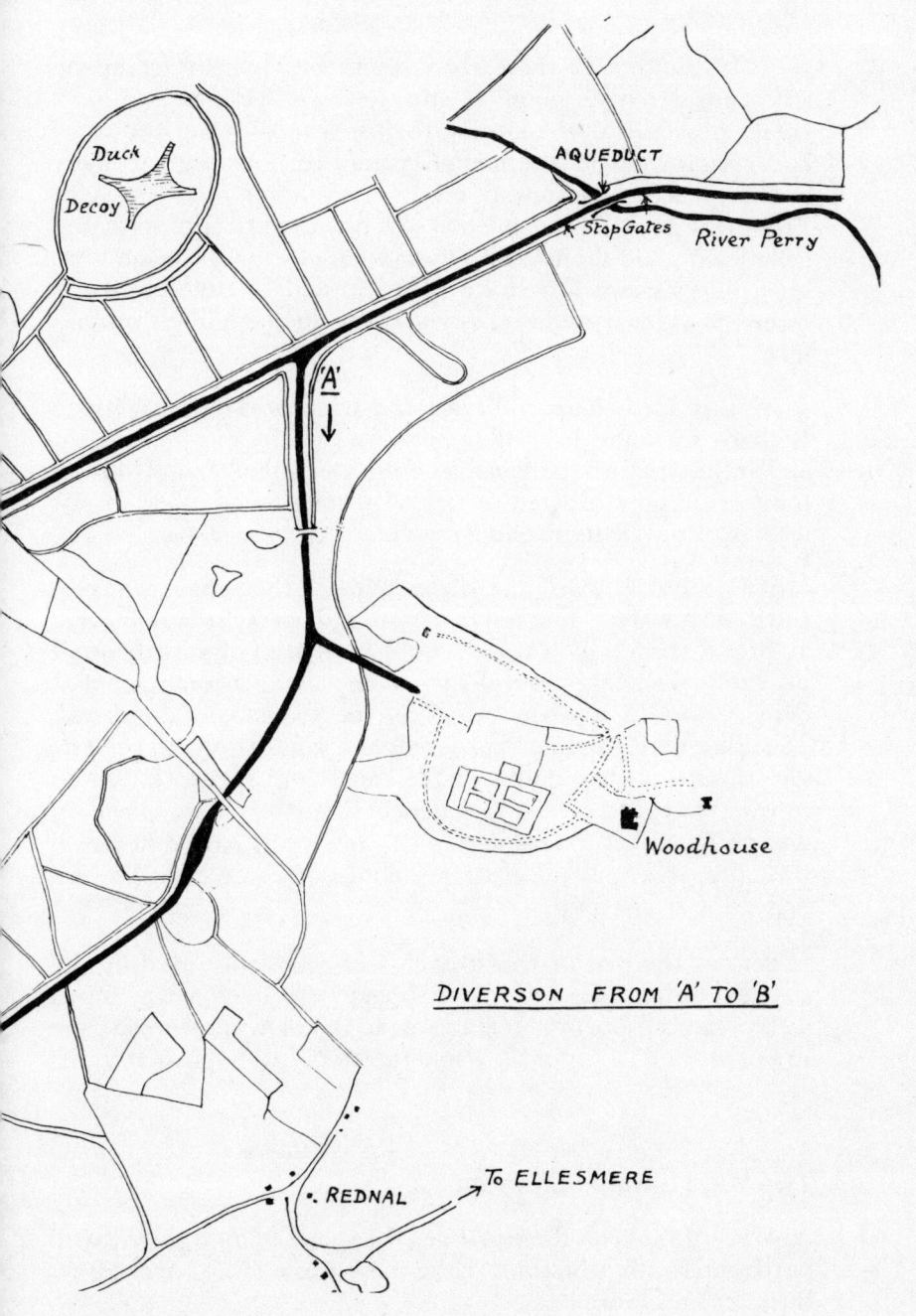

DUCK
Decoy

AQUEDUCT

StopGates   River Perry

'A'

Woodhouse

DIVERSON FROM 'A' TO 'B'

. REDNAL   To ELLESMERE

seems to be that in the early years of building the company still considered Duncombe and Jessop's Western scheme a viable possibility. According to this scheme, after the canal had climbed up to the higher ground through a great many locks, it reached the summit level of its main line at Gwersyllt. From this point a branch canal was intended to pass to Frood (or Ffrwd), and then ascend by more locks to visit neighbouring collieries and limestone quarries, and finally finish at a reservoir which would supply water for the main line's summit level.

In this area were collieries and iron works belonging to Richard Kirk and John Wilkinson, two of the most forthright and influential of the canal's committee members. It rather looks as if they insisted on an early start being made on the level portion of the Frood Branch.

We do not know if the three miles of the canal were ever filled with water. There was a basin at Gwersyllt and another at Frood from which water could have been obtained; and it probably was, for some of the colliery owners complained of damage caused to their mines by the presence of the canal. The Ellesmere Company ordered an examination 'to remedy any defects in the banks of the canal' and spent £9,000 on repairs, but there is no evidence that this short piece of waterway was ever used and only a few years passed before it was altogether abandoned, no doubt because the Western Scheme was given up.

Part of the bed of this branch was eventually used by the railway, other parts are now boggy and overgrown, but a well-preserved portion remains near Oak Alwyn, showing the towpath and a typical canal section, well grassed over.

Two Ways toward Shrewsbury

At Welsh Frankton the canal has the shape of an I girder, with north and south junctions. Here there was a fall of over 30 ft. through four locks.

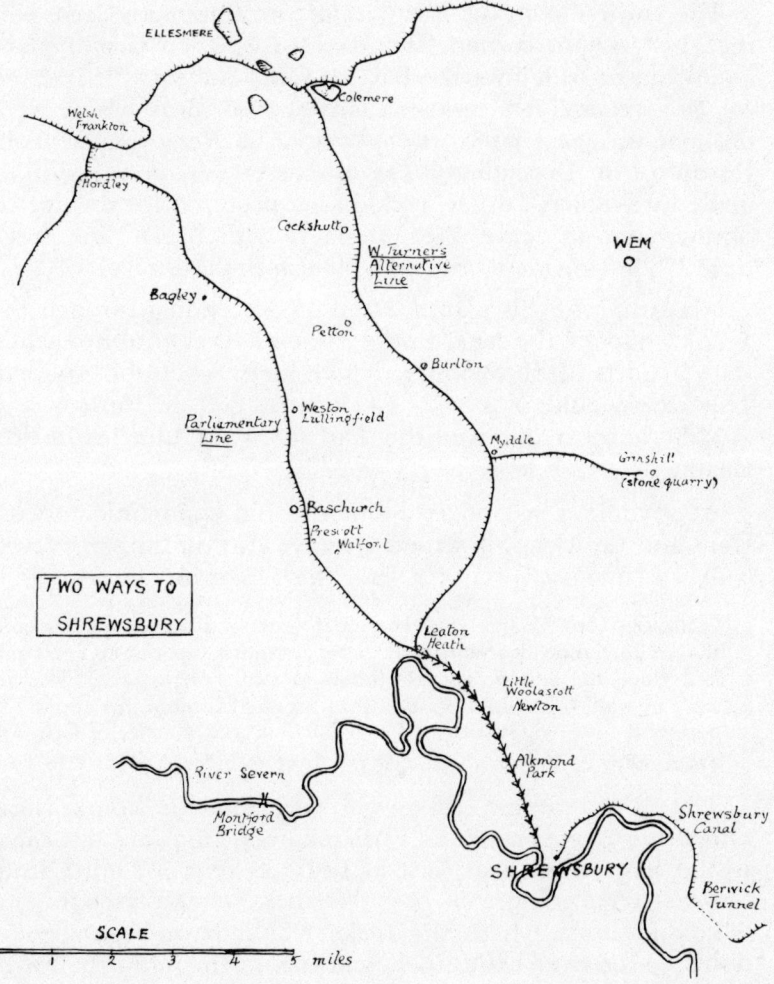

ELLESMERE

Welsh
Frankton

Hordley

Colemere

Cockshutto

W. Turner's
Alternative
Line

WEM
o

Bagley .

Petton
o

o Burlton

Parliamentary
Line

o Weston
Lullingfield

Myddle
o

Grinshill
o
(stone quarry)

o Baschurch

Prescott
Walford.L

TWO WAYS TO
SHREWSBURY

Leaton
Heath

Little
Woolastoll
Newton

River Severn

Alkmond
Park

Monford
Bridge

Shrewsbury
Canal

SHREWSBURY

Berwick
Tunnel

SCALE

0   1   2   3   4   5   miles

Today, only the northern, Llangollen Canal part of this junction is navigable. The derelict southern section was part of the waterway toward Shrewsbury.

The earliest plan for this part of the Ellesmere Canal was that by Joseph Turner, Thomas Morris, John Chamberlain and William Cowley for the Eastern Canal Scheme. It is dated 10 November 1792 and contains several ideas which were brought up again later. For instance, a *Report* by William Jessop of 8 December 1795 discusses several suggestions made by William Turner, including a proposal for the line to Shrewsbury to leave the Ellesmere-Whitchurch line (see page 17) at Colemere, instead of Welsh Frankton.

According to this plan, instead of descending through the Frankton locks, the canal would run on a level until it reached the outskirts of Shrewsbury, where locks would be grouped. This line would pass near Cockshutt, Petton, Burlton and Myddle, until it followed the 'Parliamentary Line' at Leaton Heath.

At Myddle a secondary branch would communicate with Wem and the Grinshill Stone Quarry, also on the same level. Knight's manuscript notes give the following information,

> Grinshill Stone Quarry is of the most superior siliceous quality, and that of Portland calcareous, and therefore much superior to Portland; and since the added duty is laid upon stone carried coastwise we shall be able to deliver this Grinshill Stone at London for about 2/0 per solid foot, whereas the price of Portland is 2/6, price of Grinshill Stone at the Quarry about 6d. per foot - 16 feet weight one Ton.

The River Severn follows a very sinuous course near Shrewsbury, and both the 'Parliamentary Line' and this canal would have come near to it at Leaton, some 3½ miles from Shrewsbury, going on past Woolascott and Newton to Alkmond Park, where the locks would have begun, going down to the river 120 ft. below at the north end of the town.

Besides preserving the levels, Turner's scheme also eliminated the need for a tunnel. The Baschurch Tunnel would have been 500 yd. long, and 52 ft. underground, with cuttings of 150 yd. at each end; the cost, at least £8,000. It sounds a very good scheme, but unfortunately for Turner it was turned down.

We know that the four miles of easy cutting from Hordley to Weston Lullingfields, carrying the canal's 'main line' towards Shrewsbury, were not begun until after January 1796; for only then did the following advertisement appear in the Shrewsbury Chronicle under Telford's signature, inviting tenders for,

> executing that part of the Ellesmere Canal which is now marked out, from Lower Hordley to Weston Lullingfields (a distance of four miles) . . . before the 20th. day of January 1796, and the Committee will meet at Ellesmere on the 21st. to take the same into consideration.

No special difficulties were met while extending the canal to Weston Lullingfields and building 'a wharf, four limekilns, a public house, stables, a clerk's house and weighing machine' in order to establish a centre for the distribution of lime to the local farmers. The canal was continued for about half a mile, but then it suddenly petered out in the middle of a field.

Two reasons have been suggested for this: one, that so much money had been spent so quickly that it was difficult to raise enough to build the tunnel near Baschurch and the flight of locks down to the Severn at Shrewsbury; the other, that the Shrewsbury Canal, which opened in 1797, carried limestone and coal from East Shropshire to Shrewsbury which then acted as a distribution centre, so the nearer the Ellesmere Canal was brought to Shrewsbury, the more competition it would meet.

The Ellesmere to Whitchurch Line and the Prees Branch

The canal committee originally planned for a branch to run north east from the 'main line' at Welsh Frankton to Prees, via Ellesmere which was to serve as the headquarters of the whole system (see Chapter 5). However, the Duke of Bridgewater, the first Chairman of the canal committee, not only owned the whole of Ellesmere and its surrounding countryside but also held estates at Whitchurch; and in 1795 the committee agreed to an alternative proposal that the line should extend from Ellesmere to Whitchurch, with a subsidiary branch to Prees. An Act of Parliament was obtained and work began in February 1797. However, progress was slow, as is clear from William Jessop's *Report* of 24 January 1800,

The extension from Ellesmere to Hampton Bank will tend considerably to increase the trade, and this will probably be completed within six months.

A *Report* of 25 November 1801 shows that by then only a few more miles had been added. It also shows why progress had been so slow.

From Ellesmere the canal is navigable to Hampton Bank, and it is now nearly completed to the west side of Whixall Moss; in this distance there is a tunnel, 90 yards in length, a considerable tract of lining along the sandy banks of Colemere, a portion of Moss called 'Hampton Moss' embanked to the west, and several embankments and deep cuttings to the east of Hampton Bank. Whixall Moss has been opened through its whole breadth (about 2 miles) for the purpose of draining off the water, in order to lower the surface, and consolidate the ground in the direction of the canal; this operation promises to produce the desired effects.

Having crossed Whixall Moss, the canal reached Tilstock Park in 1804 and then continued to Grindley Brook, where the level ended and wharves and warehouses were built.

At Colemere, the canal had been built on an embankment above the mere. Two advantages were taken of this: the first that two limekilns were built with their tops level with the canal towpath, facilitating the unloading of raw materials - coal and limestone - from the boats; the second was by building an 'overflow'. The canal runs for 21 miles without a lock, so its level may rise suddenly after a violent storm. The overflow allowed surplus water to run down into the mere. It was built by reducing part of the canal's bank to half its normal height above water level. This was backed by a tapering bricked gulley to a ditch running down to the mere.

Grindley Brook, where the canal ended at this time, was two miles from Sherryman's Bridge on the outskirts of Whitchurch, the authorised end of the line. The people of the town pressed for the two points to be joined, but the canal company felt there was more important work to be done and the link was not made until 6 July 1808; it then proved a mixed blessing, for the Sherryman's Bridge terminus was monopolised by one landowner, and its situation was swampy and inconvenient for building warehouses. However, the Earl of Bridgewater took down some mills in the very centre

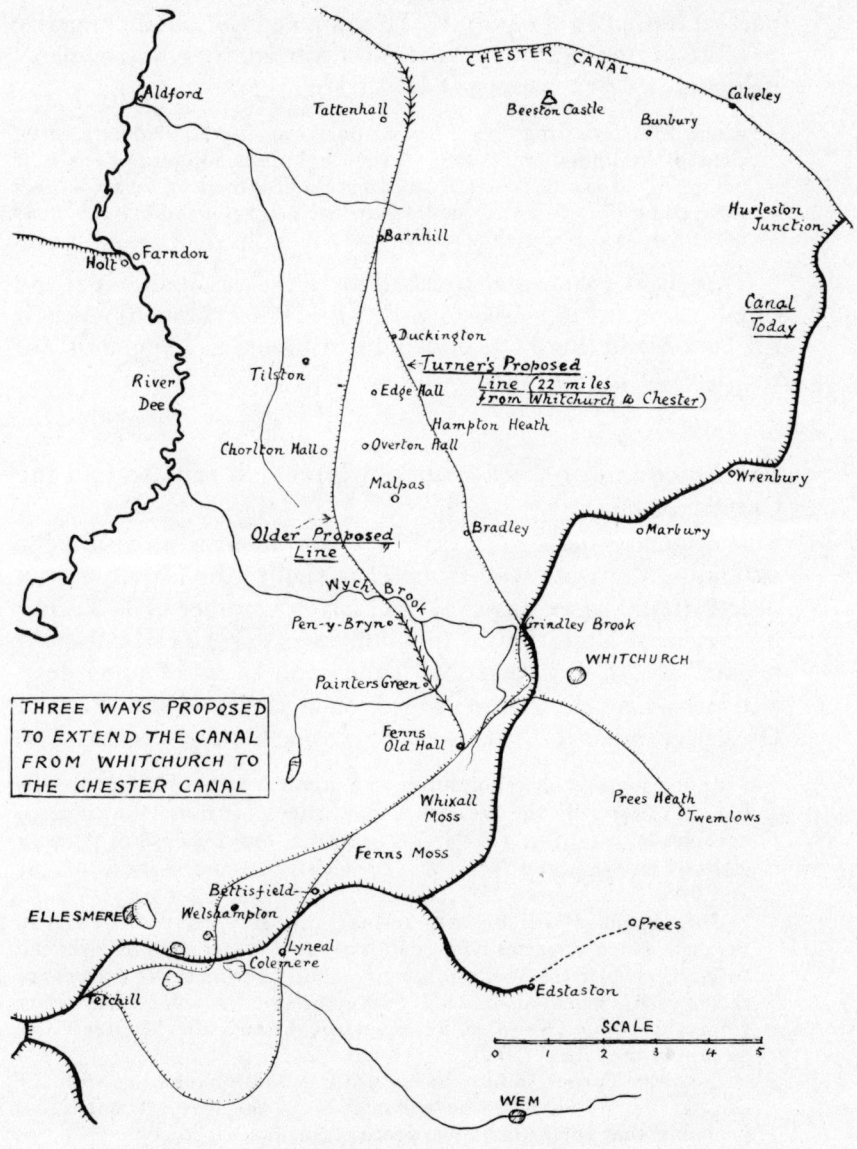

CHESTER CANAL

Aldford

Tattenhall

Beeston Castle

Bunbury

Calveley

Holt   Farndon

Barnhill

Hurleston
Junction

River
Dee

Tilston

Duckington

_Canal
Today_

←_Turner's Proposed
Line (22 miles
from Whitchurch to Chester)_

Edge Hall

Chorlton Hallo

Hampton Heath

Overton Hall

Malpas

Wrenbury

_Older Proposed
Line_

Bradley

Marbury

Wych Brook

Pen-y-Bryn

Grindley Brook

WHITCHURCH

Painters Green

**THREE WAYS PROPOSED
TO EXTEND THE CANAL
FROM WHITCHURCH TO
THE CHESTER CANAL**

Fenns
Old Hall

Prees Heath
Twemlows

Whixall
Moss

Fenns Moss

Bettisfield

ELLESMERE   Welshampton

Prees

Lyneal
Colemere

Tetchill

Edstaston

SCALE

0   1   2   3   4   5

WEM

of Whitchurch and gave the site (about 60 ft. wide) and part of a pool to the public. This enabled the canal company to extend the waterway the 400 yards from Sherryman's Bridge to a new terminus at Castle Well,

> where four boats may discharge at one time, surrounded by a wharf clear of buildings of 30 feet wide; warehouses adjoining the whole belonging to six different landowners; and a road of 30 to 40 feet wide rising only 5 feet 5 inches into the centre of the town, instead of 38 feet as at Sherryman's Hill.

This short extension, finished in 1811, was abandoned and filled in in 1944.   Meanwhile, the Prees branch reached Edstaston and there was ended, eight limekilns being built for the distribution of lime.

The Extension of the Ellesmere-Whitchurch Line to join the Chester Canal

The original Ellesmere Canal Act contained a provision for extending the waterway from Fens Hall to the Chester Canal near Tattenhall (see page 21). As early as October 1794 Turner proposed an alteration in this line to lessen the embankment needed across the Tattenhall valley and to avoid some deep cutting at Lee. He reckoned these changes would save £2,000. On 8 December 1795 Jessop, discussing Turner's plans, says,

> I cannot suppose the Committee can admit it as a substitute for the line to Chester by the Western Canal Scheme; it rests with them to consider its merits as a collateral extension; the expense of it on an estimation computed from Mr. Turner's plans and sections will be £61,395.
>
> Its advantage will be that it may probably serve the country through which it passes with coal, lime, etc., better than by a branch to Holt, part of the Western Scheme; that, of course, the expense of this branch, estimated at £13,475, may be saved; it will convey water from the summit level at Pontcysyllte through the Chester Canal to supply the Wirral Canal.
>
> But Mr. Turner thinks that two other lines of junction with the Chester Canal ought to be surveyed. On the whole I think it is probable that on future investigation this branch in some shape or other will become useful, but it can answer no purpose at present but to distract the thoughts of the Committee or their agents, while the more essential parts of the concern require their immediate attention.

Obviously, Jessop still hoped that his modified version of Duncombe's Western Scheme would soon be carried out.

The Act of Parliament which the Ellesmere company obtained in 1796 to allow it to build the Ellesmere-Whitchurch Line contained no provision for a link with the Chester Canal, so the Chester proprietors resorted to a little blackmail, cancelling their agreement to supply water to the Wirral Line. As we have seen (page 10) the Wirral Line could not function without this water. The Ellesmere committee quickly agreed to effect a junction with the Chester Canal by 1798, and the placated Chester company then restored the water supply!

The two companies agreed that the proposed junction should be altered from Tattenhall to Hurleston, and directions were given to Mr. Fletcher - for the Chester Canal Company-and Mr. Duncombe - for the Ellesmere company - to examine the countryside for a suitable route. This they did, and presented an estimate for £36,478. Far from being finished by 1798, the extension had not, it seems, begun by 1800, for on 24 January in that year, Jessop was writing 'it would be premature at present to say when the extension from Whitchurch . . . should commence'. Some cutting must, nevertheless, have been done during the following year; for on 23 September 1801 the Committee authorised one John Fletcher to start extending the canal from Church Bridge, near Marbury, to the north end of Wrenbury Common. However, two months later the Committee rescinded this order, apparently because at this point the canal would have had to withdraw water from the Steer and Cholmondeley brooks. This would have interfered with the working of several water mills and have involved the canal company in heavy compensation payments. It was decided to wait until nearer the time when the Pontcysyllte Aqueduct should be finished (see Chapter 3) before proceeding further, and the junction was not effected until 1805. Meanwhile, the Chester Canal authorities took steps to put their canal in a better state of repair since the union of the two companies' interests would soon be inevitable. However, it was not until 1813 that the companies amalgamated to become the Ellesmere and Chester Canal Co.

CHAPTER 3

THE BUILDING OF THE MAIN LINE'S
TWO GREAT AQUEDUCTS

The original Western Scheme for the Ellesmere Canal had involved crossing the Dee and Ceiriog Valleys, and while much argument was still going on about the exact route to be followed by the rest of the Line it was decided to make an early start on these two crossings in view of their great complexity. In August 1793 William Turner, John Duncombe and William Davies were asked to prepare plans for aqueducts to cross the Dee Valley at Pontcysyllte and the Ceiriog Valley at Pontfaen; and in January 1794 the committee agreed to their plans for a fairly low, three-arched, masonry aqueduct at Pontcysyllte, although this involved locks at each side of the valley to reduce its height.

On 23 September 1793 that is, a month after Turner's plans had been prepared, Telford was appointed to direct operations under the supervision of William Jessop. One of Telford's earliest tasks was to prepare the working plans and sections, and these were 'settled and approved by Jessop'. By the end of March 1794 the final specifications were worked out and James Varley, a mason, engaged to start the actual construction.

Telford was dissatisfied with Turner's plan and even while engaged on working out its specifications he was striving to find a suitable alternative. He persuaded the committee to postpone advertising the specifications until this was done, and asked them for a grant of £100 - and this was given!

At this period Shropshire was the centre of a flourishing iron industry. Abraham Darby built the first iron bridge in 1779, Wilkinson the first iron boat in 1788, and Reynolds the first canal incline in 1788. These ironmasters were keen to

24

develop new uses for iron, and as Wilkinson and Reynolds were influential members of the Ellesmere Canal Company, there can be no doubt that Telford consulted them.

During the remainder of 1794 and the first half of 1795 a revolutionary design was worked out for crossing the Dee Valley at Pontcysyllte by means of a high level iron aqueduct which needed no locks. Quoting from Jessop's *Report* to the committee on 14 July 1795, he wrote,

> It had been proposed to save expense in the Aqueduct at Pontcysyllte to reduce the height 50 feet and descend and ascend by locks, but in due consideration *I must now recommend to the Committee to make this saving by adopting an iron aqueduct at the full height originally intended* which, on correcting the levels, appears to be 125 feet above the surface of the water of the river Dee.
>
> The advantage that will attend the preservation of this level is too obvious to need explanation. The arches, or rather openings of the aqueduct, may be seven* of 50 feet each, the remainder may be raised by an embankment, and this embankment will be formed by earth to be boated from the cutting between the Dee and the Chirk Valley.
>
> It was originally proposed to cross the Chirk valley a little above Chirk Bridge but from an objection by the owner of the land, the line was altered to cross at Pontfaen. It would still be desirable to adopt the first idea, and if instead of an embankment of earth, which would shut up the view of the valley, it be crossed by an iron aqueduct I should hope the objection might be removed, as instead of an obstruction it would be a romantic feature in the view.

There is an undated entry in the financial section of the 1805 *Report*,

> William Smith, for a model of one arch of the Pontcysyllte Aqueduct   £46 - 15 - 0

and in his *Autobiography* Telford writes,

> after due consideration I caused a model to be made of two piers, a set or compartment of ribs, the canal trough, the towing path, and side railings, with all the flanches, their nuts and screws and jointing complete.

This model, made of wood, is still in existence (see Plate 14). Probably Telford had it made to demonstrate the appearance of the aqueduct to the committee.

---

* at a later stage this was increased to 18.

We would like to know who first suggested the use of iron for the aqueduct, and who was responsbile for the actual design, but it is impossible to determine either of these questions from the conflicting evidence. Let us take each claimant in turn.

1. *William Jessop.* He was the chief engineer of the Ellesmere Canal, and Telford had to get his approval for any work he wished to carry out. Further, Jessop was an ironmaster in his own right, being a partner with Outram at the Butterley Ironworks. Outram built a small iron aqueduct on the Derby Canal, which can claim to be the first one built in Britain.

In all his reports Jessop states that his recommendations to the committee are made on his own responsibility, and this would include responsibility for the iron aqueduct at Pontcysyllte. He does not give any credit to Telford for the idea. He was an unassuming man who did not court publicity, and one feels that he would have given credit where it was due. Perhaps he was assuming responsibility in case the idea was not successful.

2. *Thomas Eyton.* In Joseph Plymley's *A general view of the Agriculture of Shropshire* (1803), there is a long article by Telford on the canals of Shropshire, which is dated 1800. In it he gives the credit for first suggesting an iron aqueduct at Longdon-on-Tern, on the Shrewsbury Canal, to Thomas Eyton, the Chairman of the Shrewsbury Canal Committee. He says that the carrying out of the project was 'referred to *William Reynolds and the writer of this article'.* Reynolds was a prominent ironmaster and a member of the Shrewsbury Canal Committee.

Telford was appointed engineer to the Shrewsbury Canal on 28 February 1795; and as the masonry aqueduct at Longdon-on-Tern had been broken down by floods, it was replaced by an iron aqueduct, 62 yards long, which was finished in March, 1796, only a month after Outram's iron aqueduct on the Derby Canal.

The iron aqueduct at Pontcysyllte had already been planned, and the opportunity of building a small scale example at

Longdon-on-Tern was a godsend. Its similarity to the Pontcysyllte Aqueduct is striking, but being only 16 ft. high it was supported on iron struts, with the towpath bracketed to the outside of the iron trough. It had a fair trial, standing up equally well to the heat of the following hot summer, and the very severe frosts of the next winter.

3. *Telford.* His claims are uncertain, chiefly owing to the casual manner of his writing. We have just seen that he gave the credit for the Longdon-on-Tern Aqueduct to Thomas Eyton, a date when plans for the larger Pontcysyllte Aqueduct had already been decided upon.

In his article in Plymley's book there are two facts which are difficult to explain. First, if Telford was the originator of the idea of an iron trough aqueduct at Pontcysyllte it is strange that in this article, written while the aqueduct was being built, he should not even mention that iron was being used for it and for the Chirk Aqueduct. Secondly he includes a description of the 'Western Canal', which was never constructed, as if it was already in existence!

In his *Autobiography* (1838) Telford states that, having found the iron trough at Longdon-on-Tern practicable, '*it occurred to me* that no serious difficulty could occur in building a number of square pillars of sufficient dimensions to support a cast-iron trough, with ribs under it, for the canal.' This suggests he did not think of the iron trough idea for Pontcysyllte until *after* he had constructed the Longdon-on-Tern aqueduct! - or was it a lapse of memory after so many years?

Telford's claim to originality seems to be supported by the phrase in the last paragraph 'it occurred to me' and by a letter to Andrew Little, dated March 1795, in which Telford mentions his appointment as engineer to the Shrewsbury Canal. Concerning the two aqueducts upon it he writes,

I have just recommended an iron aqueduct for the most considerable; it is approved and will be executed under my direction upon a

principle entirely new and which I am endeavouring to establish
with regard to the application of iron.

In the same year that the Longdon-on-Tern aqueduct was
constructed, Telford built the second iron bridge to be built
in Britain, at Buildwas over the river Severn, not far from the
first one at Ironbridge. Wilkinson and Reynolds approved
Telford's plans.

There is no doubt that Telford was a quick learner, who
soon absorbed from his ironmaster colleagues the techniques
for working with iron. He went on to use iron for many
bridges, lockgates, and even a whole lock, as well as iron boats.
I am inclined to believe that he must have relied heavily on
the experience of his ironmaster friends when carrying out the
designs for the aqueducts at Longdon-on-Tern and at
Pontcysyllte.

Another puzzle is the fate of William Turner, the Whitchurch
engineer who was mainly responsible for the design of the
stone-built aqueduct. One account says that when this
was replaced, in March 1794, Turner was so disgusted that he
left the canal company. This does not square up with the
fact that (a) in a letter dated 29 April 1795, William Turner
offered to survey a line from Ellesmere to Whitchurch for the
sum of 20 guineas, and (b) he offered to survey an alternative
line which he considered was an improvement on Jessop's
Western Canal line. In the notebook of Mr. Knight (a lawyer
and committee member) we read, 'Mr. William Turner was
desired to attend Mr. Jessop on his last survey - which he did.
They proceeded from Chester on Mr. Turner's line.' This note
is dated 20 October 1795. (c) In a report from Jessop to the
Chairman of the Canal Committee several of Turner's plans
are discussed in some detail. This report is dated 8 December
1795. Thus either Turner did not resign, or, if he did, he was
soon reinstated.

When it was decided to build the Pontcysyllte Aqueduct as
an iron trough supported on stone pillars, a start was made on
the stonework immediately, and the foundation stone was
laid on 25 July 1795. James Varley had been engaged as the
contractor for the pillars, but his work did not satisfy Telford,

himself an experienced stone mason, so John Simpson of Shrewsbury was appointed to help Varley; later Simpson was assisted by John Wilson of Dalston, Cumberland. These two men were associated with Telford for the rest of his life. Another of Telford's stalwart assistants was Matthew Davidson. He had come from Telford's birthplace, Langholm in Scotland, to superintend the building of Montford Bridge in Shropshire, and was then engaged as superintendent at Pontcysyllte. The canal company built a cottage for him at the north end of the aqueduct, and he superintended the masonry work in a most satisfactory manner.

In early correspondence the aqueduct is spoken of as having eight arches; but as confidence grew, no doubt as a result of Telford's success at Longdon-on-Tern, the number of pillars at Pontcysyllte was increased to 19, thus shortening the length of the earthern embankment. Most of the earth for this embankment came from the extensive cutting which was being done adjacent to the Chirk Tunnel, and as soon as the canal was cut between here and Vroncysyllte the earth was boated to the site of the aqueduct. William Davies, another local man, made a very successful job of the embankment which was said to be one of the largest earthworks built in the 18th century.

The Chirk Aqueduct was begun on 17 June 1796, later than the Pontcysyllte Aqueduct, but it was finished well before it, in 1801. The reasons for this were twofold; firstly, it was not so difficult to construct; secondly, its completion including that of the tunnels and cutting up to Vroncysyllte, added another four miles to the canal, tapped the coal from the Black Park Colliery, and allowed coal and iron from north of the Pontcysyllte Aqueduct to reach the canal after a short land carriage.

The ten arches of the Chirk Aqueduct, each of 40 ft. span, are more solidly built and wider than those of Pontcysyllte. This resulted from the manner of the building of the aqueduct, details of which are given in Telford's *Autobiography*,

The spandrills of the stone arches were constructed with longitudinal walls instead of being filled with earth, and across these the canal bottom was formed by cast-iron plates, at each side infixed in

square masonry. Those bottom plates had flanges on their edges and
were secured by nuts and screws at every juncture.

The sides of the canal were made waterproof by ashlar masonry
[i.e. squared stone-work] with hard, burnt bricks laid in Parker's
Cement, on the outside of which was rubble stonework [i.e. somewhat
irregular quarried stone embedded in mortar] like the rest of the
aqueduct.

The width of the waterway is 11 ft., of the masonry on each
side 5 ft. 6 in., and the depth of the water in the canal is 5 ft.

A *Report* of 27 November 1799 includes the following
information,

All the arches of the aqueduct at Chirk are now completed, and the
spandrels, and wing walls, with the preparations to receive the bottom,
will be ready in the Spring; proposals for the iron plates, which are
to form the bottom, have been received, and they will be provided
and laid early next Summer.

The Minutes of the company for the same date state that
William Hazeldine's estimate for the ironwork should be
accepted - his charge on delivery was ten guineas per ton.
It is rather puzzling why iron was only used for the bed of the
aqueduct, whereas in both the Longdon-on-Tern and Pontcysyllte Aqueducts it was used to make complete iron troughs.
A further puzzle is that today Chirk Aqueduct *does* possess
an iron trough, although no reference to the date of the
changeover has come to light as far as I know.

A progress report to the General Assembly, dated 25
November 1801, mentions the completion of the Chirk
Aqueduct, and goes on to report,

At the north end of the aqueduct there is a tunnel 460 yards in
length which (except for a final proportion of towing-path) is also
completed - to form this tunnel, the ground, though deep, was cut
open in different lengths, which afforded an opportunity of making
the brickwork very perfect, and securing the top of the arch with
clay and loose stones, to prevent the waters of the upper strata from
injuring the work; by this means, if any water flows from the hill,
it will fall into the canal and a very considerable quanity now falls in
from the strata cut through by the tunnel.

To the north of the tunnel, the deep cutting which continued for
about threequarters of a mile, and was a tedious operation, is now
finished, and will be ready for navigation about Christmas.'

Concerning the Pontcysyllte Aqueduct a postscript to the
1799 *Report* informs us,

It was also ordered that the works at Pontcysyllte which have for some time been suspended to expedite those at Chirk, be proceeded with as soon as the weather will permit in the Spring.

The next *Annual Report*, dated 5 February 1800, presented by Jessop, shows that at last the idea of the Western Canal Scheme was being abandoned,

> It is wholly inadvisable to execute a canal between Pontcysyllte and Chester, and especially since the extensive opening of the collieries between Harwarden and Flint, which communicate by railways with the Dee, so as to deliver coal at much less price at Chester than formerly - the great object for immediate consideration is, how to deliver coal at the least expense from the Ruabon Collieries, into the basin on the south side of the Dee at Pontcysyllte.

The Report goes on to say that even if a canal was built for this purpose there would still have to be railways [i.e. horse-drawn tramways] from the individual collieries; and owing to the nature of the ground the canal would need many locks. Jessop reckons the cost of a railway would be half that of a canal, and so recommends it.

He then puts forward the surprising idea that if a railway was built it might be continued over the aqueduct to the far side of the valley at Vroncysyllte. The cost of a railway viaduct as compared with an aqueduct would be £8,400 less, notwithstanding the £500 expense of conveying the water across in elm pipes; also the time taken to build a viaduct would be one year less, which would mean an increase in revenue. The waggons used would be connected by lengths of chain. Further it was pointed out that if at a later date it was decided to revert to an aqueduct once more, this could be done quite easily.

Suggestions are made about the masonry work (probably Telford's ideas); the piers, built of ashlar masonry, were solid up to a height of 70 ft., and above that hollow. In his *Autobiography* Telford says of this design,

> The outer walls being only two feet in thickness, with one cross wall, not only places the centre of gravity lower in the pier and saves masonry, but ensures good workmanship, as every side of each stone is exposed.

Jessop puts in a word of praise for Telford, 'I cannot leave Pontcysyllte without saying that the columns, without any exception, are executed in a more masterly manner than anything of the kind that I have before seen.'

The 1801 *Report* describes the work on the Pontcysyllte Aqueduct one year after the Chirk Aqueduct had been completed,

> During the last year and a half five piers have been built from the foundations up to the level of 110 feet above the common surface of the river Dee. Nine other piers have been raised 23 feet in height, which has brought them to the same level; there are five other piers which require 23 feet each to raise them to the before-mentioned level.

Notice that the number of piers had now been extended to 19, whereas the *Report* of 1795 gave the number of arches as seven.

The next year's *Report to the Assembly,* dated 30 June 1802 tells us that navigation by boats was now possible from Chirk Bank right up to the basin at the south end of the embankment leading to the Aqueduct. Further, that in anticipation of the completion of the canal works several new collieries had opened in the neighbourhood of Ruabon and Plaskynaston. It definitely had been decided to connect all these with the basin at the northern end of the aqueduct by a tramway, and work had already been authorized for its construction in June 1801.

With the stone piers of the Pontcysyllte Aqueduct virtually completed tenders for the iron work were invited and on 17 March 1802 Hazeldine put in his successful bid for the castings at £11 per ton and for 'wrought iron at 8d. per pound, and being allowed £30 for cast iron keys to connect the plates of the aqueduct, over and above the price of £11 per ton.' The total cost of the iron work is given as £17,284; while the iron rails, etc., needed for the Pontcysyllte tramway came to £3,643; and there was a further sum of £220 for the cost of iron work, rails and waggon wheels needed for the work on the construction of the earthern embankment.

1804 was a very busy year, as it was proposed to open the Aqueduct before the end of 1805, and it was hoped that work on the extension of the canal to the river Dee at Llantisilio (i.e. the 'Water Line') would be finished at the same time. 500 workmen were employed on these projects. With regard to the Aqueduct the *Report* of 28 November 1804 states:

The iron work of the trough-part of the Aqueduct of Pontcysyllte over nine arches is now put up, being nearly one half of the whole length; many plates being now cast and brought to the bank at the north end of the aqueduct - the workmen being familiar with the operations of putting the plates together - and the operations at the Foundry being a very regular train and well supplied with metal, there is reason to expect that the whole of the trough-part will be completed about Midsummer next.

Timber has been provided for a part of the towing path, which will be put early in the Spring, as well as the iron railings to protect it. The earthen embankment and lining of the canal is now carrying on by means of three iron railways; and it is proposed to have this part finished at the same time with the Aqueduct.

In order to have a plentiful supply of coal the Committee have taken measures to make a cast-iron double railway from the basin near the north end of Pontcysyllte, through the Acrefair, Plas Madoc and Plas Benyon Collieries; and Mr. Hazeldine has undertaken to deliver the iron rails upon the spot, of the best quality, at eleven pounds per ton, and to maintain the same for twelve months after they are laid.

The Opening of the Pontcysyllte Aqueduct

After ten years the Pontcysyllte Aqueduct was ready for use, and its ceremonial opening took place on 21 November 1805, only one month after Nelson's famous victory at Trafalgar.

The Committee were determined that its time schedule should be adhered to, in spite of the fact that the 'Water Line' was far from complete. Water from the Tref-y-nant brook must have been utilized as a temporary measure.

The following description of the opening is culled from eye-witness accounts.

The Aqueduct had been filled, and just before 2 o'clock the procession began from the basin at the Vroncysyllte end. The first boat carried the Earl and Countess of Bridgewater and other important proprietors, with a serjeant-major of the Shropshire Volunteers in full dress uniform stationed in the bow bearing an elaborate flag. The committee and Thomas Telford were in the second boat; the third carried the band of the Shropshire Volunteers in full uniform playing patriotic airs; the fourth was reserved for the heads of departments and others connected with the work; while the last two boats which were to bring coal back, carried an assortment of people anxious to be amongst the first to cross the Aqueduct.

As soon as the first boat entered the cast iron waterway, the Artillery Company of the Shropshire Volunteers fired 15 rounds from the two brass cannon, which had been captured from Tippoo Sahib at the battle of Seringapatam, and had been presented to the Company by the Earl of Powis; while the multitude of people watching from the surrounding hills broke out into cheers.

As the boats entered the basin on the north side of the Aqueduct, five waggons drawn by one horse, and containing two tons of coal each - the produce of Mr. Hazeldine's collieries at Plaskynaston - were brought along the iron tramway and deposited on the wharf so that the coal could be loaded into the last two boats. The passengers then landed and at a nearby house belonging to the company 'partook of a cold collation' and listened to an oration specially written for this occasion.

After re-embarking, the procession returned in the same order, followed by the two boats laden with coal, while the 8,000 people repeated their cheers, the band played martial airs, and the cannon fired another fifteen rounds. On the return to the Vroncysyllte basin a reception was held, and then some of the people proceeded along the canal and through the tunnels, the head and stern of each boat being lighted by torches.

CHAPTER 4

THE TWO MAIN INDUSTRIAL CENTRES
OF THE CANAL

The 1805 *Report* said that the canal's main purpose was to serve the agricultural community and its chief revenues were expected to be derived from this source (see Chapter 1, p.1). However, the industrial Wirral Branch was far more successful than had been anticipated and its terminus, Ellesmere Port, rapidly developed into a flourishing commercial centre. Another prosperous industrial area developed around the Pontcysyllte Aqueduct when a tramway was built between it and the Ruabon and Wrexham coalfields. The growth of these two industrial centres will be discussed in this chapter.

Ellesmere Port

As the most important trading-centre on the canal, Ellesmere Port handled an ever-increasing volume of traffic. The impression given by the Company's Reports and Minutes is misleading. They emphasise the expenses and difficulties of maintaining the port and sound like excuses for running at a loss, but in fact Ellesmere Port's revenue increased every year between 1795 and 1805 - by which time it was paying a dividend of 5% - and it continued to expand throughout the 19th century. Its profits helped to finance the early stages of the building of the rest of the canal. In 1821, a committee was appointed to examine the whole of the canal to find out whether any economies could be introduced in order to increase the revenue still further. In its report we find that the north piers and the tide lock at Ellesmere Port had just been rebuilt and the walls of the tide basin and other parts of the port had been repaired. In 1843 £100,000 was spent on the construction of a new, large dock 435 ft. long and 139 ft. wide. The opening of this dock did not take place quite according

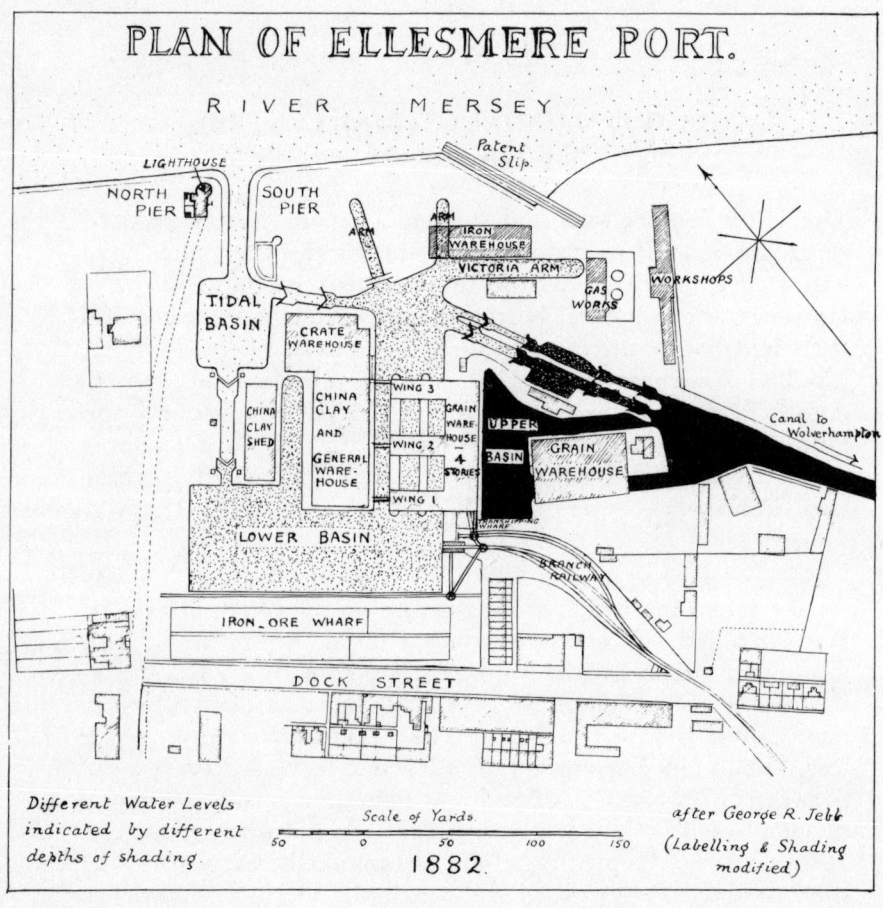

PLAN OF ELLESMERE PORT.

RIVER MERSEY

Patent Slip.

LIGHTHOUSE

NORTH PIER

SOUTH PIER

ARM

IRON WAREHOUSE

VICTORIA ARM

GAS WORKS

WORKSHOPS

TIDAL BASIN

CRATE WAREHOUSE

WING 3

GRAIN WAREHOUSE

UPPER BASIN

Canal to Wolverhampton

CHINA CLAY SHED

CHINA CLAY AND GENERAL WAREHOUSE

WING 2

4 STORIES

GRAIN WAREHOUSE

WING 1

LOWER BASIN

TRANSSHIPPING

BRANCH RAILWAY

IRON ORE WHARF

DOCK STREET

Different Water Levels
indicated by different
depths of shading.

Scale of Yards

50   0   50   100   150

1882.

after George R. Jebb
(Labelling & Shading
modified)

to plan. It was intended to mark the occasion by the ceremonial entrance of the steamer, the *Earl Powis,* into the dock. The steamer had been decorated with flags and banners and carried two small cannon. When the chairman, Earl Powis, other members of the committee, and guests had embarked, the lockgates connecting the new dock with the old tide lock were swung aside; the band got ready; the crowd prepared to cheer - and then came the anti-climax; the steamer was just a few inches too wide to go through the lock! However, the important people soon transferred to the 100-ton schooner, *Bridget,* of Liverpool, and she made the entrance successfully, followed by five or six other vessels, amidst the cheers of the people, while the band, playing patriotic airs, marched around the quay.

As always on these ceremonial occasions, the opening was followed by a liberal dinner of roast beef, pork, goose, etc., washed down with plenty of good liquor. Nearly 500 workmen had their meal in the upper storey of one of the big warehouses, and each was supplied with a pint of beer free of charge. The more important people had their meal served in the lower storey, and, no doubt, had a more delicate choice of things to eat and drink.

The prosperity of the port depended on the development of certain industries. A plan, dated 1882, shows a China Clay shed and warehouse. China Clay was an essential constituent in the making of pottery, and most of it came from Cornwall. Although railways were developing, small coasting vessels were still the cheapest means of transporting it to the Mersey, where it could then be transferred to canal boats at Runcorn, to go to the Potteries directly by the Trent and Mersey Canal, or at Ellesmere Port to go to Chester, then by the Chester Canal to Barbridge, where the Middlewich branch connected up with the Trent and Mersey Canal at Middlewich.

The Corn-milling Industry developed greatly as the Canadian prairies were opened up and became one of the largest wheat growing areas in the world. Three large flour mills and a very large grain elevator were built at Ellesmere Port.

The first mill to be built was known as the Imperial Flour Mill. It began operations in 1905, ran until 1929 and then stood idle until 1940, when it was started up again to help to replace the milling capacity of certain mills destroyed by enemy action. After the war it was taken over by Ranks, who ran it for a short time while some of their own mills were being re-built. Then, in August 1962, it was bought by Criddle and Co., who continue to use it for the manufacture of compound animal feeding stuffs.

The King Flour Mills started up in 1906 and ran continuously until April 1970, when it was closed down following the amalgamation between King Flour Mills Ltd. and W.O. & J. Wilson (millers) Ltd., the production of both mills being centred in a new mill built on the site of Wilson's old one.

The third mill was built by F.A. Frost & Sons in 1906, to replace their old Chester Mill, and was the biggest of the three mills at Ellesmere Port. It closed down in the early 1950s, its production being transferred to the larger dockside mills at Birkenhead. Six years ago it was taken over by the Ellesmere Port Storage Company for use as a general warehouse, but it was almost completely destroyed by fire on 28 June 1970.

The grain supplied to the mills was practically all imported, most of it coming via Liverpool and Birkenhead, but some via Manchester; and then it was delivered to the mills in barges of between 100 and 150 tons' capacity, travelling along the Manchester Ship Canal to Ellesmere Port and then along the mill arm from the lower basin. The main sources of supply were Canada, U.S.A., Australia and the Argentine, but a certain amount of grain came from India and Russia. Flour was distributed to Chester, Stoke-on-Trent, Wolverhampton, Birmingham and other Midland towns.

There was also a considerable trade in iron ore and iron. The 1882 map shows an iron ore wharf and also an iron warehouse which cost £10,292 to build. A photograph of 1906 depicts a row of waggons being loaded at the wharf with iron ore from Cumberland. A lot of iron from blast furnaces in Staffordshire, Shropshire and North Wales travelled along the canal, while its Middlewich branch carried iron from North Wales to Manchester.

Boat-building was another activity carried out here, although for relatively small boats and barges only. There are two methods adopted for building boats; one is to build the boat in a 'dry dock', so that when finished the boat can be 'launched' simply by letting water into the dock - most narrow-boats were built in this way; the other is to build the boat on a sloping slipway, and when finished allow it to slide down the slipway into the water.

At Ellesmere Port the slipway method was used and it was of a type described by Telford in his *Autobiography* as Moreton's Patent Slip. Iron rails were laid down on each side of an even slope, with a cogged rail down the centre. A very wide wooden trolley ran on these rails and was positioned some way up the slope, and the boat constructed or repaired on it. When finished, the trolley with the completed boat was allowed to run slowly down the rails until it entered the water and the boat floated off. Some years ago the slipway was still in a usable condition, although the trolley was so broken as to be hardly recognisable; later the rails were removed. Mr. Hewitt, at one time Inspector at the Ellesmere Depot, used to work at Ellesmere Port canal basin until the Manchester Ship Canal leased it in 1921, and he remembers when the slipway was in use for repairing boats.

When the Manchester Ship Canal was built it ran along the coast in the neighbourhood of Ellesmere Port, and its outer wall had to be specially constructed. This meant that the old entrance from the Ellesmere Canal's tide basin, which formerly entered directly into the Mersey, now entered the Manchester Ship Canal, so that boats had to proceed along this as far as Eastham Locks to get out into the Mersey. This happened first on 16 July 1891.

A recent industry, centred at Stanlow adjacent to Ellesmere Port, is the Petroleum Industry. Not long ago the experiment was tried of using narrow boats as 'tankers'; they were decked over and filled with petroleum products at the modern refinery, and sent in pairs to the Midlands via Ellesmere Port and the canal - but the experiment did not last long.

We are so used to thinking of canal boats as freight carriers that it comes as rather a surprise to learn that as soon as the Wirral Line was opened a boat was put on for carrying passengers. The *Shrewsbury Chronicle* of 19 June 1795 states,

> On Wednesday last the first Canal Packet Boat on the Ellesmere Canal began plying between Chester and Liverpool. The fare being only 2/6 for passengers, will, no doubt, bring plenty of custom to the Proprietors. The Gentlemen of the Ellesmere Canal Committee, we hear, will not suffer their servants to take any money or other gratuities from passengers. The boats are ordered to set out from Chester just two hours before high water, to prevent passengers being unnecessarily delayed.

At Ellesmere Port the passengers changed to a larger boat to cross the Mersey to Liverpool. In the company's Minutes for 26 November 1800 we are told that Elizabeth Coffield proposed paying the company £300 per annum as rent for navigating the boat used between Ellesmere Port and Liverpool, the company requesting 'that a room or apartment be made as a resting room for ladies, and that the packet boat be always immediately cleaned as soon as the passengers are discharged; and this Committee insist upon Elizabeth Coffield always keeping three sober, steady and able men at least, on board the packet to navigate the same.'

Another Minute for 23 September 1801 states that Samuel Akerley 'proposed to rent from the Company the Ellesmere Port Canal Tavern and the *two* packet boats with the profits of serving passengers therein on the Canal from Chester to the River Mersey at the clear yearly sum of £1,000 for the term of two years'.

These quotations seem to show that passenger carrying was a profitable business, and we know that it continued until at least 1834; but the *Report* for 1821 refers to the need for immediate repairs to Caughall Bridge and carries the following grisly note - 'Many accidents have happened and some lives have been lost by the Packet Boats passing under bridges.'

An even more surprising piece of information is that in 1823 Charles Hickson, who then ran the Ellesmere Port-Liverpool boat, advertized that he had fitted up baths, shower baths and bathing houses for women, and a newly fitted hotel for those who desired to lodge there during the bathing season. Today a less likely place for a bathing resort could hardly be imagined!

This part of our story has a sad conclusion for no commercial traffic now plies the Wirral Line. Modern ships cannot pass through its narrow entrance into the canal basin. Indeed, some modern oil tankers are so big that they cannot even enter the Manchester Ship Canal, and the new Queen Elizabeth Dock has been built for them at its entrance.

It is this side of Ellesmere Port which now flourishes. Quite large vessels pass along the Ship Canal to Manchester on the one hand, and on the other, to Eastham Locks where the Ship Canal enters the Mersey. Here are wharves, warehouses, powerful electrically-operated cranes and a floating dock which can accommodate sizeable ships. But at terminus of the Wirral Line, the warehouses are empty, Telford's arched warehouses have been destroyed by fire, the wharves are deserted and the railway lines becoming hidden in grass. British Waterways has closed its offices and toll house. There are no boats in the lower basin and only pleasure craft in the upper one. Yet the town of Ellesmere Port was created by the Wirral Line and the prosperity of the modern city is its fitting memorial.

The Pontcysyllte Area

As we have seen in Chapter 1, a number of the original canal proprietors favoured the Western Canal Scheme, which would take the waterway through the industrial region around Ffrwd, Bersham, Brymbo, Wrexham and Ruabon, on the North Wales coalfield. When this scheme was finally abandoned, it was decided to build a tramway from the Ruabon area to join the canal at the Pontcysyllte Aqueduct, where a short northern extension was made to the canal, ending in a double dock shaped like the prongs of a tuning fork. Coal, iron, limestone, bricks, etc., could now be carried along the tramway to the canal. This encouraged the sinking of more coalmines and the establishment of further industries.

One of the most important works already established in the area was William Hazeldine's Plaskynaston Iron Foundry. It was opened in about 1800 and, although the cast-iron arches for the Aqueduct were made at Hazeldine's Coleham

works, the remaining castings needed for Pontcysyllte were
made at the Plaskynaston Foundry, which also provided the
iron bed of the Chirk Aqueduct, the lockgates at the western
end of the Caledonian Canal, the Betws-y-coed 'Waterloo'
bridge and the Conway and Menai suspension bridges.
Hazeldine still owned the foundry in 1835 but by 1853 it had
become the property of Moss and Jukes. In 1856 William
Hughes was the owner and continued to work at Plaskynaston
for the rest of the 19th century. The works were active until
the 1930s. They were demolished in April 1947 by their new
owners, Monsanto Chemicals, who needed the site for further
development (see page 46).

In the early 19th century, a number of industries on the
Plaskynaston estate were owned by Exuperius Pickering.
By the 1820s he needed to transport coal from the Plas-
kynaston Colliery to his limeworks and ironworks and so had
the canal extended by a small branch, sometimes called the
Plaskynaston Canal. A tramway linked it to the colliery.

In the second half of the 19th century we find the main
employers here were the collieries, T.E. Ward's ironworks
and the New British Ironworks, but there were also a number
of smaller factories including:

The Plaskynaston Tube Company. Also known locally as
the 'Pipe Works' this is known to have been operating in
1874. About 100 men, women and children were employed,
and they manufactured iron pipes 20 ft. long, the iron
strips required being obtained from the New British
Ironworks. A boatload of pipes left by canal each night.

Sylvester & Co. Plaskynaston Screw-bolt Works. Although
working in 1874, these works do not seem to have been
very successful, for they are not mentioned in a directory
for the area, dated 1880.

Boiler-making Works. Situated near the railway station at
Acrefair, near the spot used later by the chemical works
for loading and unloading, it was active in 1874.

Plaskynaston Potteries. Little is known about this works
although a directory of 1869 refers to the manufacture of
'glazed earthenware', and the factory is shown on the

Ordnance Survey map for 1873. The path through the chemical works to Queen Street was always referred to as the 'Potteries Road'.

The Old Soap Works. Probably manufactured carbolic and soft soap and flourished about 1890.

Ben Hughes Brickworks. In 1874 this works was manufacturing fireclay goods, bricks and chimney pots, and possibly household ware.

J. C. Edward's Brickworks, Trefynant. First recorded in 1856 and closed in 1964 when the site was acquired by Monsanto. Bricks, fireclay articles and terracotta were made.

It was into this environment that Robert Graesser, a German immigrant, came in 1867. He went into partnership with a Manchester lawyer, Timothy Crowther, at the Plaskynaston Chemical Works at Cefn Mawr, close to the northern end of the aqueduct. They started with only three employees. After a quarrel the partnership was dissolved and Graesser set up on his own in buildings close by.

The works were known locally as the 'Oil Works' because the chief process carried out was the extraction of paraffin oil and wax from shale, a waste product of the local collieries. There is a road which still bears the name of 'Oilworks Road'.

With the opening of the American oil wells prices slumped, but Graesser was a determined and resourceful man, and he turned to the distillation of crude tar acids, in order to obtain pure phenol and cresylic acids. He was so successful that within five years he was successfully competing with Germany, and by 1880 was providing more than half the world's supply of the highest quality phenol.

In those days tar and its crude distillation products were classed as noxious substances, and their carriage by road or rail was forbidden; thus Graesser obtained his 'coal tar acids' by canal from the Midlands, and the refined products reached consumers by the same route.

Graesser continually improved his plant, and by 1887 had virtually rebuilt it three times and boosted output from 20 tons to 1,000 tons a year. Additional products made were:

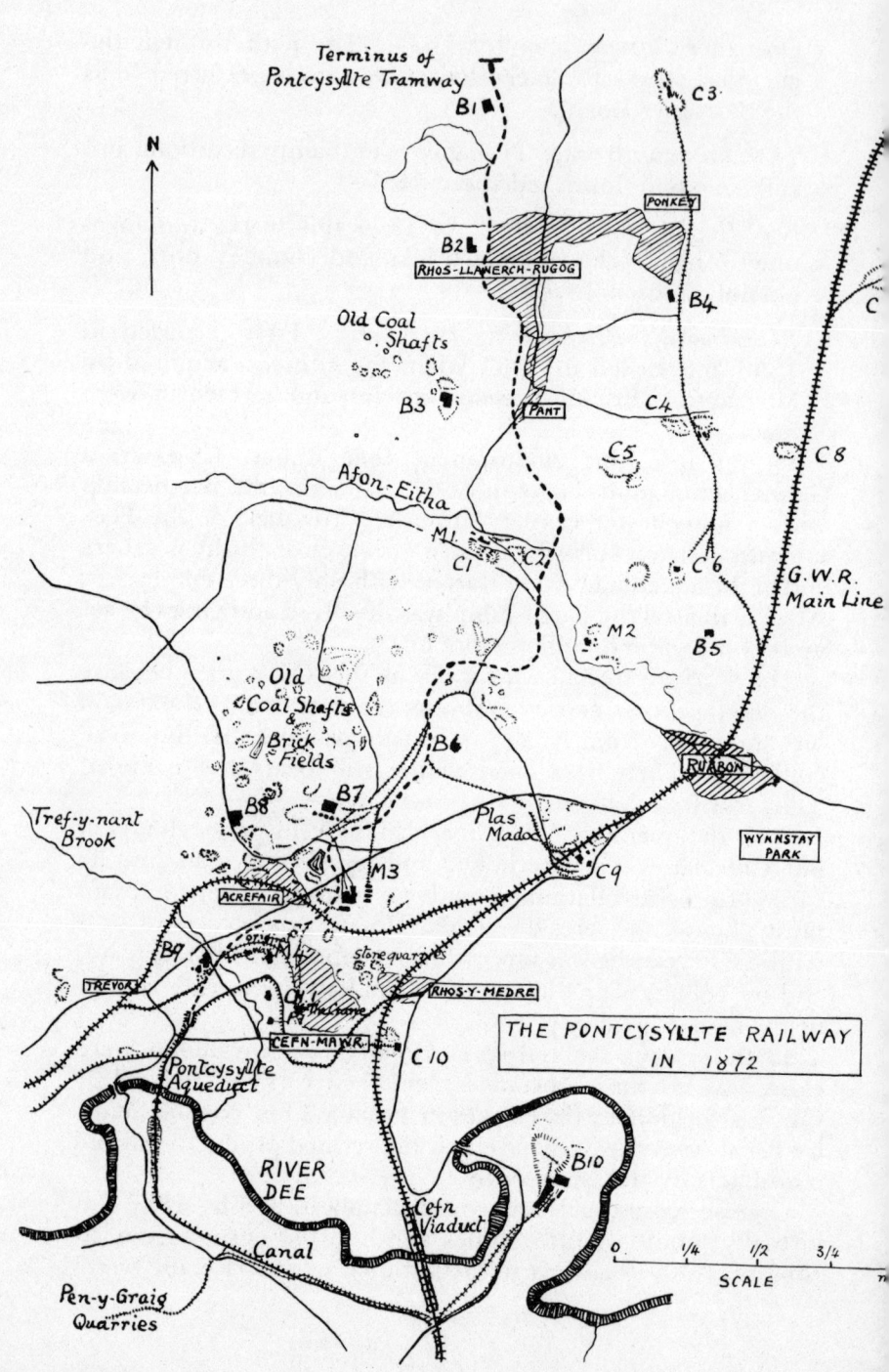

THE PONTCYSYLLTE RAILWAY
IN 1872

KEY TO MAP

- - - - - - - - Pontcysyllte Railway
(originally a tramway)

++++++++++++++ G.W.R—Shrewsbury-
Chester Line

++++++++++++++ Other tramways and
feeder railways

―――――― Roads

LIST OF WORKS OPERATING IN 1872

BRICK WORKS

B.1. Lwynn Einion
B.2. Rhos
B.3. Pant
B.4. Ponkey Brick & Tile Works
B.5. Tatham Brick & Tile Works

B.6. Plâs-yr-Wern
B.7. Delph
B.8. Penbedw Fireclay Works
B.9. Tref-y-nant Fireclay Works
B.10. Pen-y-bont Brick & Tile Works

COLLIERIES

C.1. Plâs-Bennion
C.2. Wynne Hall
C.3. Bryn-yr-Owen
C.4. Brandie
C.5. Gardden

C.6. Gardden Lodge
C.7. Hafod-y-Bwch
C.8. Vauxhall
C.9. Wynnstay
C.10. Plâs-Kynaston

METAL INDUSTRIES

M.1. Wynn Hall Spelter Works
M.2. Ruabon Foundry (Iron & Brass)

M.3. New British Iron Works
M.4. Plâs Kynaston Foundry (Iron)

CHEMICALS

CH.1. Plâs-Kynaston Chemicals

POTTERY

P.1. Plâs-Kynaston Pottery

an orange dye, aurine, derived from phenol; and a yellow dye, picric acid, which was also used in the manufacture of the explosive, *Lyddite,* used during the Boer War.

Graesser died at his desk in the factory in 1911, but the business was continued by his son. It did valuable work during the first World War.

In 1901, in St. Louis, Missouri, John Francis Queeny began the manufacture of saccharin. His works were named 'Monsanto' in honour of his wife, whose maiden name was Monsanto.

In 1920 Queeny bought a half share in the Cefn works, and it was renamed the Graesser-Monsanto Chemical Works. The production of saccharin, vanillin and aspirin was added to the chemicals manufactured. Also at this time came the development of synthetic resins (plastics) for which phenol was needed.

In 1928 the Graessers severed their connection with the works, and in 1934 it became a public company known as Monsanto Chemicals, Ltd. From now on, the number of new products made makes an impressive list. In 1935 phthalic anhydride and benzoic acid plants went into operation; a sulphuric acid plant was installed in the same year. The next year saw new plants for making phenacetin, phthalic esters, and rubber chemicals. The phthalic anhydride used for making benzoic acid and sodium benzoate was also used in the fast growing paint and plastic industries.

The research laboratory is ever seeking to keep Monsanto in the forefront of organic chemical manufacture, such as the use of silicon in the electronics industry and new ways of making modern plastics.

In 1946 a £750,000 expansion programme commenced with the purchase and demolition of the old Plaskynaston Foundry. A commemorative plaque is all that marks the site of the old works. Today, some 200 products are made by Monsanto and their main works at Cefn Mawr are so close to the better known town of Ruabon that these are referred to as the Ruabon Works.

These big changes occurred around the southern limit of the Pontcysyllte Tramway. The original tramway ran along Oilworks Road, through the present Monsanto Works to the north and east of the Plaskynaston Canal as far as the 'Crane', so called because the difference in level necessitated the transference of goods by means of a crane. When it was decided to extend the tramway northwards the new line started from the Crane. However, at a later date (probably when locomotive traction was introduced) a shorter, more level route was made by building a stone-faced embankment northwards across the Trefynant Brook, and ran just over four miles going through Rhosllanerchrugog and finishing just past the Llwyn-Einion brickworks, about ¾ mile south of Legacy. Many works developed along its course or were connected to it, at first by a horse-drawn tramway, and later by a single-track, standard-gauge railway line.

In 1872, to the northwest of the New British Iron Works, with its coke ovens, we find the Penbedw Brickworks and other similar works, situated amidst a landscape bespattered with the spoil heaps of former collieries and brickworks. It was here that the drying and packing of the dangerous picric acid was carried out during the first World War.

The railway then ran along an embankment which became increasingly higher until it assumed impressive proportions. Well below, a meandering stream, called the Afon Eitha, was carried through the embankment by a substantial tunnel lined with terra cotta bricks. It was quite lofty, about 24 feet high. While the roof was semicircular in section, its bed formed a shallow curve lined by stone blocks. The embankment was about twice as high as the tunnel. The original tramway probably ran further to the west, the embankment being made when locomotive traction was introduced.

Immediately to the west were the Wynne Hall Colliery and the Plas Bennion Colliery, as well as the Wynne Hall (Kenrick's) Spelter Works. Still further northwards the railway passed by Pant (with its brickworks) and then by Rhosllanerchrugog (with more brickworks), and it finished just beyond the Llwyn-Einion Brickworks.

Slightly to the east we find other works connected up by a common tramway which joined the main G.W.R. line just north of Ruabon. These included the Bryn-yr-Owen Colliery, the Ponkey Brick and Tile Works, Tatham Brick and Terra

Cotta Works, Brandie Pits, Park Pit and Gardden Lodge Collieries, with the Ruabon Foundry (Iron and Brass) and the Gardden Lodge Quarries not far distant.

On the G.W.R. main line further collieries were present, namely the Hafod-y-Bwch and Vauxhall, north of Ruabon, and the Wynnstay and Plaskynaston Collieries to the south.

The Pontcysyllte Tramway was still horse-drawn in 1862, but by the end of 1861 conversion to a locomotive line began, although it was not finally completed until January, 1867. In 1879 the extension beyond Afon-Eitha went out of use, and in the 1880s works adjoining the railway began to close down - in 1882 Kenrick's Spelter Works were closed, and in 1887 the New British Iron Company, one of the main users of the railway, went into liquidation, Thus, when the G.W.R. introduced a bill for a railway from Wrexham to Rhos they offered to buy the line, and actually did so in February, 1896, at a cost of £51,000. Under the terms of the agreement, the G.W.R. were empowered to adapt the line for passengers as well as for freight traffic. Two trains a day were run to the wharf at Pontcysyllte and differential rates in favour of canal carriage were maintained.

In this century there was a gradual slackening of the use of the canal and of the Pontcysyllte Railway, little business being done after the First World War.

CHAPTER 5

ELLESMERE AND WELSH FRANKTON

A glance at the map of the canal system on page 4 shows clearly that Ellesmere was its natural focal point. The canal proprietors' 1805 *Report* says,

> The Committee have judged it necessary to erect a Canal Office at Ellesmere, being the most central point in the Navigation. This will contain a Committee Room, an Office for Accounts, and another for Plans etc., also apartments connected herewith for the resident Accountant Agent, and the resident Engineer.

The Canal Office, built in 1806, a house of ample size and dignity, stands at the junction of the canal's three branches. The Committee Room was the ground floor of a semi-circular wing commanding views in three directions, towards Chirk, Nantwich and, along the canal's short Wharf Arm, to the town of Ellesmere itself. Today the Office is divided into five flats and never within living memory has it been used as business premises. Two magnificent copper beeches at the entrance to its front drive give the Office its present name, Beech House.

Adjacent to the house stands the Canal Maintenance Depot. This is now run by only a skeleton staff, as British Waterways has centralised its maintenance work for this area at Wigan; yet as recently as 1948 the Ellesmere Depot employed nearly 30 men, engaged in maintaining a wide area of the Shropshire Union Canal, of which the Ellesmere Canal is now a part. In its early days the depot also housed the canal's central workshops.

Lockgates were built from baulks of oak, and towards the end of the depot's active life these were bought ready-cut. In earlier days, however, they had been sawn by hand on the spot, and the filled-in site of the depot's saw-pit can still be

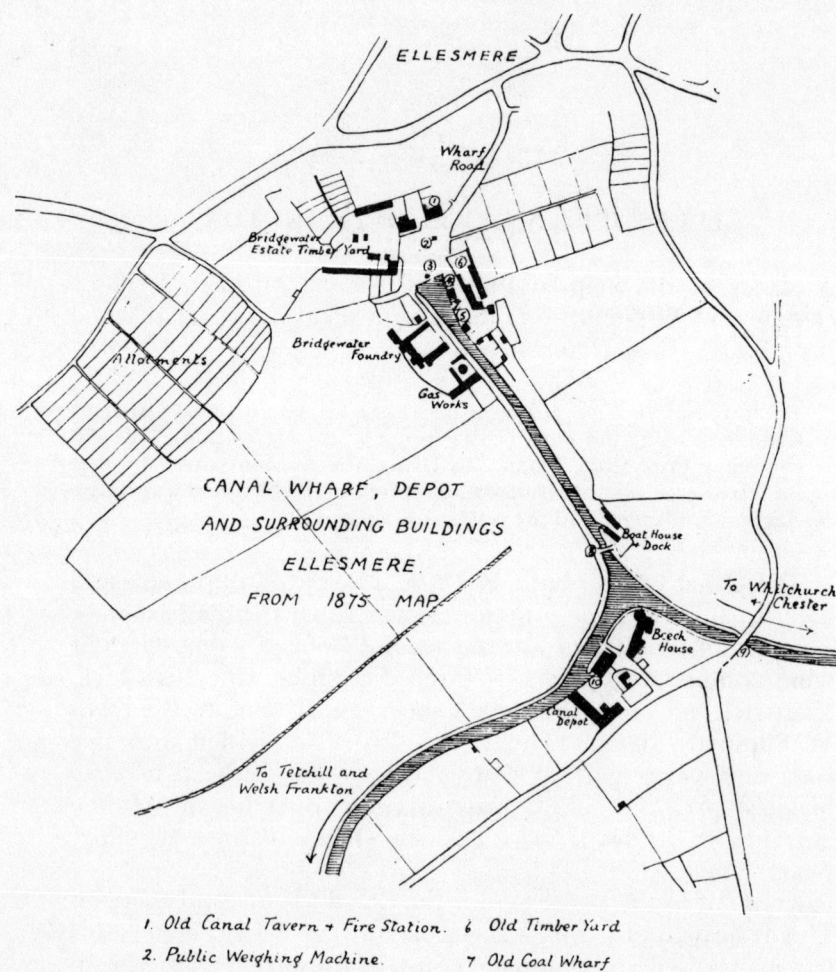

ELLESMERE

Wharf Road

Bridgewater Estate Timber Yard

Bridgewater Foundry

Gas Works

Allotments

CANAL WHARF, DEPOT
AND SURROUNDING BUILDINGS
ELLESMERE.
FROM 1875 MAP.

Boat House Dock

To Whitchurch + Chester

Beech House

Canal Depot

To Tetchill and
Welsh Frankton

1. Old Canal Tavern + Fire Station.   6. Old Timber Yard
2. Public Weighing Machine.   7. Old Coal Wharf
3. Old Crane.   8. "White Bridge" – a Roving Bridge
4. Large Warehouse.   9. "Red Bridge".
5. Smaller Warehouse.   10. Dry Dock for boat building + repair

traced. The pit was about 6 ft. deep and 15 ft. long. Oak trunks were supported across it and sawn up by two men, one standing on the edge of the pit, the other on its floor, smothered in sawdust. Their positions signified their relative importance: the 'top sawyer' was the man in charge.

The iron parts of the lockgates were prepared in the depot's smithy. Even 20 years ago this seemed a museum piece, its walls hung with an astonishing display of old-fashioned tools, but the antiquated air was dispelled by a glimpse of the workshop's electrically operated bellows.

Upright members of the lockgates were mortised by hand, using a mallet and chisel. The crossed members were then tenoned in and sometimes a diagonal one added to give extra strength. They were secured with large nuts and bolts. Sometimes the holes for these had to be enlarged with a red-hot rod, a process which filled the lockgate shop with smoke.

When finished, the gates, weighing several tons apiece, presented transport problems. One large gate made in 1948 for the Leeds and Liverpool Canal was too big to go through the canal bridges and tunnels so it had to be sent by road. However, the lane from the Ellesmere depot was too narrow to allow its passage, so the gate was taken by boat to the canal wharf, and there loaded on to a lorry. It was interesting to listen to the workmen discussing the problem of how to get the gate to the wharf, and to watch them carry out their plan of bringing up a narrow boat, placing two baulks of timber across it and gently lowering the lockgate, balancing it carefully, before towing the boat to the wharf.

There were many other woodworking jobs to be done at the depot, besides making lockgates. The yard housed a carpenter's shop, a paint shop, and a pattern-maker's shop producing the hard, wooden patterns needed to make the many pieces of cast-iron used along the canal. Some of these patterns were beautifully finished artefacts, carved by a craftsman who obviously took pride in his work. When finished they were sent to Clay's Iron Foundry on the canal's Wharf Arm and there used to make the sand moulds in which the iron was cast. This pattern-maker's shop was closed

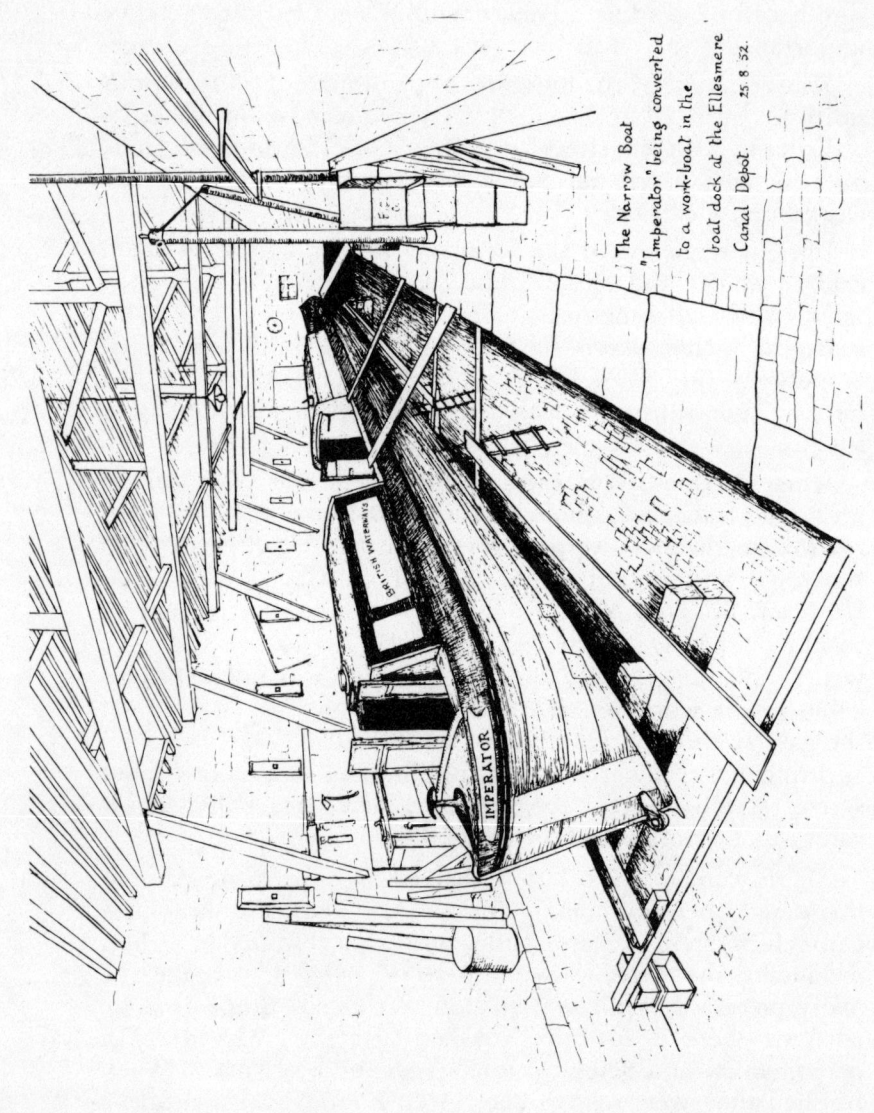

The Narrow Boat
"Imperator" being converted
to a work-boat in the
boat dock at the Ellesmere
Canal Depot.   25.8.52.

Plate 1.—Ellesmere Port in 1906. Tide lock leading to Lower Basin, with a freighter and three-masted schooner

Plate 2.—Telford's warehouses at Ellesmere Port, built on arches to preserve the level from the upper basin warehouses—note footbridges. These warehouses were destroyed by fire

Plate 3.—Black Park dock inlet from canal. Old photo (1904?) of a narrow boat by the wharf where roadstone, slate, etc., were loaded, having been brought by the G.V.T. (note rails and horse-dung). Also chain hanging from crane, and towpath bridge over Black Park coal-dock inlet

Plate 4.—Repair work on the Ellesmere Canal near Wenffryd Bridge. Sept. 1945. A break occurred in the bank on 7 Sept. 1945, washing away part of the railway track just below. Note the workmen relining the canal bed with puddled clay, and the trucks, rails and excavator in the distance

Plate 5.—Longdon-on-Tern iron aqueduct. The first iron aqueduct of any size in the world. Was 60 feet long, and was a try-out for the very much larger Pontcysyllte Aqueduct

Plate 6.—Chirk Tunnel entrance. 16 Jan., 1952

Plate 7.—Telford's Chirk Aqueduct, and Robertson's railway viaduct beyond it, where they both crossed the valley of the river Ceiriog. 16 July 1970

Plate 8.—Chirk Aqueduct. Workmen from the Ellesmere Depot cleaning out the Aqueduct. Notice the stop-planks in position; the entrance to the tunnel beyond; and railway viaduct to the left. After removing silt, scale and rust by burning, the ironwork is protected with bituminous paint

Plate 9.—Pontcysyllte Aqueduct, viewed from the river bed level. 16 July 1970

Plate 10.—Wooden model of one arch of the Pontcysyllte Aqueduct, 12ft. x 4ft. x 2ft—made before 1800. 26 Aug. 1956

Plate 11.—Looking south along the Pontcysyllte Aqueduct when the trough was emptied for repairs. The wooden planks hide the tow-path, but the latter's supports and railings are well shown. 24 Jan. 1972

Plate 12.—Pontcysyllte Aqueduct. We cross it in the 'Beryl'. Note the hilly country, the narrowness of the canal trough, towpath and iron railings on one side only. 17 Sept. 1952

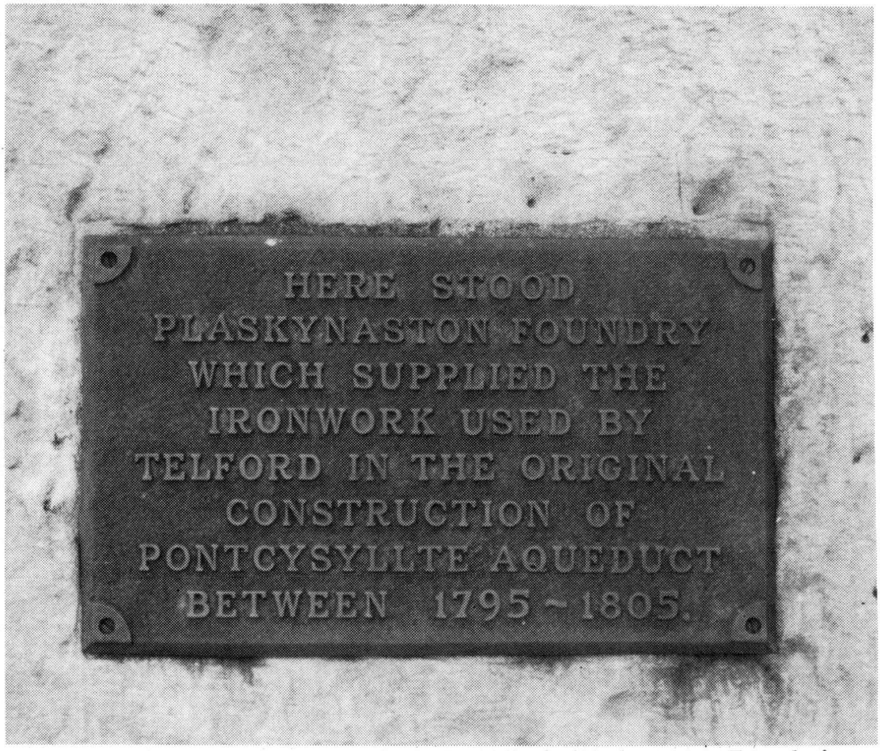

Plate 13.—Plaque on spot where Hazeldine's 'Plaskynaston Foundry' used to stand—now inside Monsanto's Works

Plate 14.—Morris's 'Lift-up' bridge across canal at Whixall Moss.
8 July 1950

Plate 15.—The Horse-shoe Weir at Llantisilio, beyond Llangollen, where the water from the river Dee enters the Ellesmere Canal. 1964

Plate 16.—Canal pleasure cruisers at the Ellesmere wharf arm of the canal

before 1948, but its room, filled with patterns, showed how self-supporting the depot used to be.

20 years ago, the depot yard was dominated by a massive overhead crane. Its uprights of tall square-sectioned baulks of timber supported equally large, horizontal beams. The frames ran down each side of the yard to overhang the water's edge - producing the effect of a colonnade. The wooden frame supporting the crane hut was stayed with iron rods. It extended across the yard and ran on small wheels along the crane's outer members. A few years ago this crane was condemned as unsafe and replaced by an imposing iron jib-crane, but this came too late to be of any real use as little work is now done in the depot. Another item which has now disappeared is an engine adapted from a locomotive engine, the cylinder and piston being mounted vertically. It came from Crewe and generated power for working the machinery.

An inlet from the canal led to the Boat Dock where boats were once built, repaired and 'indexed'. A Mr. Moody, whose father and grandfather also had worked on the canal, had once been in charge of the building of several narrow boats, but by 1948 only repair work was being carried out in the dock. The boat to be repaired was floated in and then a dam built across the entrance by dropping 'stop-planks' into iron-shod grooves. The water was then drained out, the boat coming to rest on baulks of timber in the now dry dock.

I saw one narrow boat, the *Imperator,* undergoing extensive repairs, including the renewal of the stern (stem-post) and considerable lengths of planking. To join the stem-post the planking had to be bent into a curve. This was done by steaming it for several hours in a steam chest. Once removed the wood had to be worked rapidly before it cooled down again, as only for a very short time would it bend without splitting. Stout strips of iron were later fastened to it to make a secure job.

Every few years all boats had to be caulked. Narrow boats are flat bottomed, and elm planks two and a half inches thick are fastened across the bottom of a boat at right angles to its length. To make sure that the hull is water-tight, frayed out rope or hemp is forced into the cracks between the planks by means of a short, cold chisel with a flattened

COPPER INDEX STRIP

Marked in tons and half tons, and having a strip at the top marked with the date and the number of the job

SET OF STAMPS USED AT THE ELLESMERE DEPOT FOR MARKING COPPER INDEX STRIPS

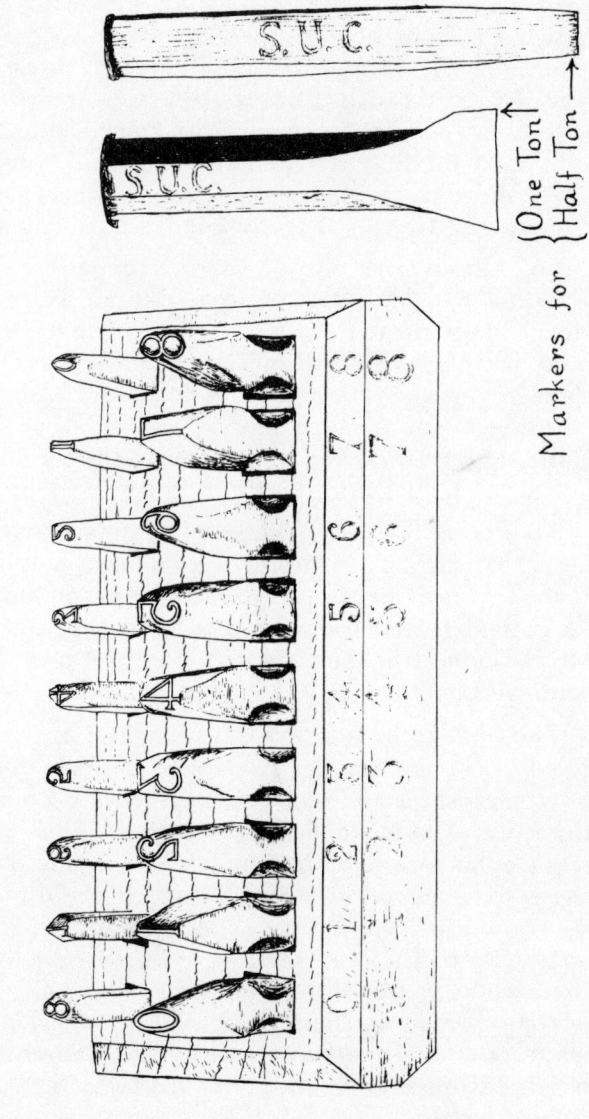

Markers for {One Ton / Half Ton}

edge. It is hit with a special caulking hammer shaped like a letter T, and made of iron wood, lignum vitae or other very hard wood. The hammer is swung in a wide arc against the chisel, the boat being tipped up on one side to give ample room for the swing. In order that the hemp shall not be forced right through the crack, the bottom boards are backed with long planks, fixed at right angles; the same principle applies to the long side-planks of the hull, which are backed with short vertical ones. The caulking process is then completed by giving the whole hull a coat of tar.

Mr. Moody was one of the boat repairers who was quite at home with an *adze*. This is like an axe with the sharp-edged blade turned at right angles to the haft. It was often used astride the work between one's legs, which sounds a dangerous operation and, in fact, Mr. Moody recalled an occasion when an adze slipped and cut the workman's leg. Quite unperturbed he walked over to the tar pot and brushed hot tar on to the cut before continuing his job!

Tolls were levied by the canal company on the weight and nature of the cargo carried, and all boats had to be 'indexed' to make it easy for this weight to be determined. The method of indexing used today differs from that used in the past. Mr. Moody, who has a notebook recording the indexes of some 50 boats, recalled the older method.

The boat to be indexed was brought empty into the water-filled dock, and vertical grooves were made in the hull at the bow, amidships and stern on each side to accomodate laths; these were lightly nailed in position. Four heaps of large, rectangular iron weights were piled alongside the dock, where there were two cranes each of which could pick up weights from two of the heaps. Each crane lowered two tons, consisting of three 600 lbs. weights and one 440 lbs. weight for each ton; thus four tons were added altogether, spaced out equally along the length of the hull. Marks were then made on the six laths at water level. Further four tons of weights were added, and marks made, until the boat held 28 tons of weights.

The weights and the six laths were removed and the four ton markings subdivided to give one ton markings. The permanent markings were made on copper strip, by placing lath and strip side by side and stamping the figures from one to 28 tons, using a special series of steel stamps. The six numbered copper strips were then fastened to the hull in the grooves already present. There were six of them to obviate any difference which might be due to uneven loading resulting in the reading at one end being too high and that at the other end being too low; by taking the average of the six readings an accurate reading was bound to result.

The men were not only employed at the depot itself, but also along the line of the canal. Besides the lock-keepers (often living in one of the company's cottages) there were 'length men' responsible for a certain length of the canal. It was their job to prune the bushes and trees alongside the towpath, scythe the grass, check that the towpath and canal bank were in good order, keeping a keen eye for signs of any trouble such as an incipient breach in the bank. If a break did occur it was their duty to fix stop-plank dams on either side of the break to prevent more water escaping. Such stop-planks were heavy boards, with a lifting ring at each end, and they were kept at bridges in wooden shelters, usually seven in each shelter. The canal narrowed down at the 'bridge-holes' and had vertical brick sides with stone capping, so that it was easy to fix vertical iron-shod grooves into which the stop-planks could be placed. (In recent years the wooden shelters have been replaced by ugly structures made of concrete having an iron door at each end). While the damaged portion of the canal was being repaired, quite a number of men from the yard would be employed on the job. Other jobs might include the clearing of weeds, dredging, cleaning out an aqueduct, the installation of a new lockgate, the repair of bridges or of a collapsed culvert, etc.

The early prosperity of this part of the Ellesmere Canal was linked with its position on the Earl of Bridgewater's estates. The Earl was not only the canal's first Chairman but owned the whole of Ellesmere itself, and his estates were self-supporting. At Haughton, only a mile to the north of Ellesmere, the Earl set up brick-works. At the Ellesmere Canal Wharf he built a large timber yard, a carpenter's shop,

paint shop and other worksheds where wood for fencing and
for his cottage and farm buildings was prepared. At one side
of the Wharf stood the Bridgewater Iron Foundry (more
generally known as Clay's Iron Foundry) producing iron
castings not only for the Bridgewater estates but also for the
canal. One Ellesmere man, now over 90, recalls working at
this foundry; but its site has long been incorporated into the
buildings of Unigate Dairies, and milk tankers now unload in
what was once the foundry's central yard.

Inevitably, the canal wharf became the commercial centre
of the town. At the Wharf the canal company owned a
three-storey warehouse from which, no doubt, many of the
goods transported by the waterway could be bought. Next to
it stood a smaller warehouse with Nunnerley's coal wharf in
between. A bill head of 1834 shows what a variety of goods
was then sold at the wharf. It reads,

> R. & J. Tilston, who have constantly on sale, Memel, Riga, Dantzic,
> and Pine Balk; Norway, Scaffold and Ladder Poles; Red and White
> Deals, Laths, Slates, Tiles, and Buckley Mountain Drainage Pipes,
> etc., etc., Oaks, etc., Timber, Oak Gates, Hurdles, and all kinds of
> Wheelwrights and Coopers Stuff; Roman Cement; Boat Builders,
> Tarpawling, and Mill-sail Makers; and Vendors of Canvas, Rope,
> Pitch, Tar, etc.

The rope would have come from the Rope Walk behind the
houses of Charlotte Row (this is shown on old maps). The
pitch and tar would have been obtained from the gasworks
which had started in 1832 along the canal's Wharf Arm.
Boat building was carried out at a privately owned dock by
the footbridge (White Bridge) at the entrance to the Wharf
Arm. This dock was part of a two-storey building, the dock
itself being at canal level, while the upper storey served for
carpentry and stores.

In 1846 the Ellesmere Canal became part of the Shropshire
Railways and Canal Company. This name is still clearly
visible, painted on the end wall of the canal company's
warehouse. It is followed by the words, 'General Carriers to
Chester, Liverpool, North and South Staffordshire and
North Wales'. Later the canal was taken over by the L.M.S.
railway, as the railway crane still standing at the head of the
Wharf reminds us. Here too there used to be a weighing

machine, but that has disappeared. The former *Canal Tavern* has become a private house, and the adjoining garages mark the site of the town's old, manually operated, fire station.

The history of Ellesmere is full of surprises. Today the town has no connection with brewing or with the malting industry, but 100 years ago there were two breweries here. The Ellesmere and Vyrnwy Brewery stood at the top of Market Street. Later it was taken over and developed as the Rennet Works. The other stood behind the old Town Hall and was later demolished.

In Samuel Bagshaw's *Gazetteer of Shropshire* (1851) Ellesmere, which had a population of 2,000, is listed as having 21 public houses. The Rev. John Peake (vicar) observed in his personal notes (unpublished MS.) that the most difficult situation he met was refusing to partake of home-brewed ale at every house at which he called; other members of the local clergy were less particular and literally reeled their way home!

When the railways were about to be introduced to the town a witness to a Parliamentary Committee was asked if it were true to say, 'Ellesmere is only second to Newark in the importance of the Malting trade'. He answered, 'Yes'. Answering another question this witness stated there were 'Thirty malt houses in and around Ellesmere in 1861.' Today, even the last remaining malt house has recently been demolished. It stood behind Owen's furnishing shop in Cross Street.

Much of the malt was sent to Lancashire. Since it was a perishable commodity it received priority treatment and was dispatched from the canal wharf in 'fly boats'. These were narrow boats of unusually light build, and travelled fast. They had right of way at bridges and locks, sometimes sounding a horn to give notice of their approach. They were served by a double crew, two men working by day and two by night. The boats paused only at locks or when changing horses, and fresh animals were held in readiness for them at regular intervals along the way.

Whereas Ellesmere was once the centre of malting and brewing, it is now important for making cheese and this by no accident. Shropshire, like Cheshire, has long been known for its dairy herds and its cheeses. These were formerly made by farmers' wives, who took them to the nearest market town's Cheese Fair. Older people in Ellesmere can remember these fairs, when horse-drawn carts stretched from the church to the market place as their owners waited for their cheeses to be assessed and bought. There were always a number of Lancashire dealers at this fair, and in order that their cheese should arrive in the best condition it too was despatched by 'fly boat' from the canal wharf.

Towards the end of the first World War, one George Stokes was given the task of persuading local farmers to sell their milk instead of making cheese on the farm. The reason was that, due to the sinking of food ships by German submarines, there was insufficient cattle food available to City dairymen who had kept milking-cows on their premises, to claim that milk was sold 'fresh from the cow'. Many farmers soon began to sell their milk, but as few farms are close to the canal, barges could not be used to bring the milk to the new dairy on the old foundry premises by the Canal Wharf. The foundry had closed down a few years earlier because its famous Cockshutt ploughs, named after the village on the Shrewsbury road, could be made more cheaply in the Black Country.

Dairy machinery was installed to cool the milk brought warm from the farms by mule-drawn wagons and, later, by solid-tyred lorries. For the long journey to London, the old Cambrian railway was used. By 1919 the dairy's owners Great Western and Metropolitan Dairies, Ltd., had merged to form United Dairies, parent of Unigate. More milk became available than was needed for London housewives, so George Stokes, a native of Cheshire, naturally turned to making Cheshire Cheese to utilise the surplus. From these small beginnings cheese making has increased yearly so that many tons are now made each day behind the well preserved foundry facade. These cater not only for cheese-making but also for the conversion of the by-product, whey, into a more concentrated form and its ultimate use as a food.

Welsh Frankton
As the site of Unigate's large factory, Ellesmere is still important, whereas Welsh Frankton has reverted to the quiet

village it was in the days before the canal was thought of; but in the early 19th century it must have bustled with activity as boats on Ellesmere Canal's four main branches met here. To the *Canal Tavern* came boatmen travelling with coal and slate from Ruabon, limestone from Llanymynech, timber and wheat from Ellesmere Port and timber and agricultural produce from Weston Lullingfields.

The canal installations at Welsh Frankton were interesting and are shown on the map on page 62. Just after the bridge at the north junction, on the Ellesmere side was a wharf with a finger post pointing to 'Newtown', 'Chirk', 'Llangollen' and 'Chester'. Here too stood a warehouse and crane. The warehouse was demolished in the 1940s and the material used to build a bungalow at Lyneal for the canal's District Inspector.

Proceeding southwards along the 'link' part of the junction one reached a double lock, i.e. two locks with a common intermediate gate. Owing to the sharpness of the canal's fall here, the gate was very tall. It and a small footbridge across the lockgates still stand. At the head of the first lock the original gate has been replaced by a concrete barrier. Nearby stands the Check House, where the weights of the narrow boats' cargoes were read off from the boats' index strips (see page 56) and appropriate tools charged. The old *Canal Tavern*, now a private house, may be seen to the right of the pound immediately after the double lock.

On the far side of the canal a lane leads down to what was once the lock keeper's house and the stables where the draft horses for the boats were kept. Beyond the third lock is a boat-building dock, workshop and cottage. Their age is uncertain but Bagshaw's *Gazetteer of Shropshire* gives 'William Jenks, boat builder' at Welsh Frankton in 1851. It was at this dock in the 1920s that the *Cressy*, L.T.C. Rolt's famous boat, was repaired for its former owners, the Peates (see page 93). Today, however, the site is derelict. The entrance from the canal has been walled up and the dock itself houses a few hens and plenty of weeds. Stone steps lead down into it, and on its floor stand two stone baulks which once supported boats when water was emptied through the sluice gates.

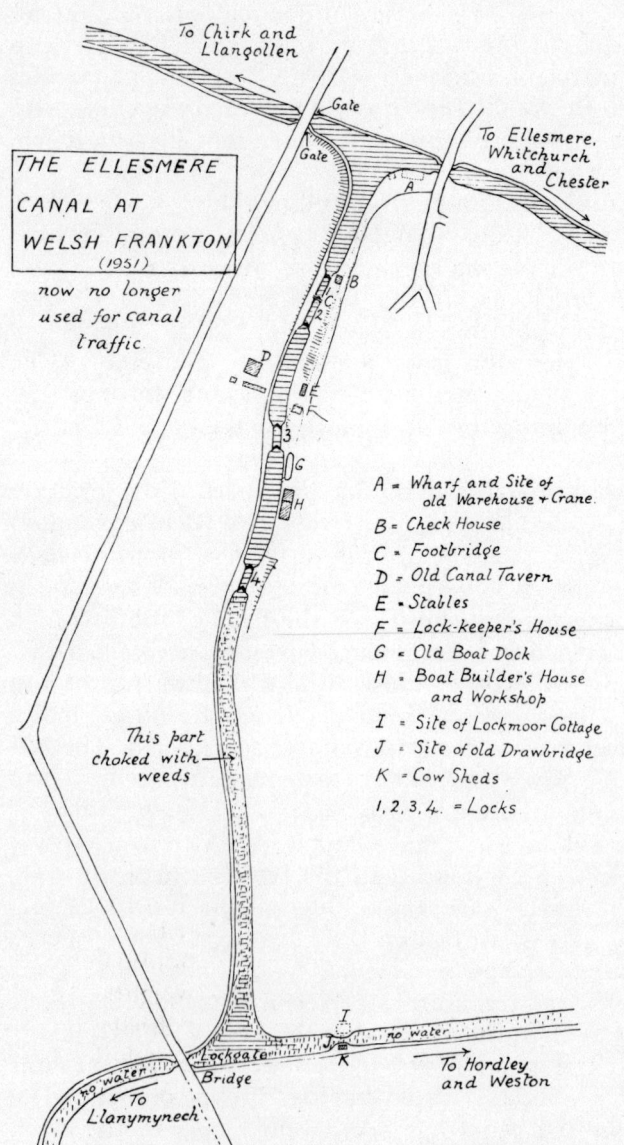

To Chirk and
Llangollen

Gate

Gate

**THE ELLESMERE
CANAL AT
WELSH FRANKTON**
(1951)

now no longer
used for canal
traffic

To Ellesmere,
Whitchurch
and Chester

A

B

C

2

D

E

F

3

G

H

This part
choked with
weeds

A = Wharf and Site of
  old Warehouse + Crane.

B = Check House

C = Footbridge

D = Old Canal Tavern

E = Stables

F = Lock-keeper's House

G = Old Boat Dock

H = Boat Builder's House
  and Workshop

I = Site of Lockmoor Cottage

J = Site of old Drawbridge

K = Cow Sheds

1, 2, 3, 4. = Locks

I

no water

Lockgate
Bridge

K

To Hordley
and Weston

no water

To
Llanymynech

Part of the former workshop has been converted into an extension of the cottage and practically all traces of the original equipment have gone. All that remained in 1951 was a pair of bellows, 7 ft. long, which must have been used to blow the forge fire.

Half way along the junction link stands the fourth lock, followed by a stretch of the canal now almost completely blocked by rushes, reeds, sedges and other marsh plants; and on either side of the southern junction's terminal pool, now filled with reedmace (bulrush), the canal has been drained. One can now walk for miles in the direction of Weston Lullingfields, in part along the almost dry canal bed and in part across fields where the canal has been bull-dozed out of existence.

Along this line in 1951 Shade Oak Bridge was demolished; a few years later Sycamore Bridge went; and about 1960 Hordley Bridge; while the basin adjacent to Hordley Bridge was filled in, obliterating the wharf there. A burst in the bank at Dandyfield in May 1917 was the excuse for limiting the navigation to Hordley Wharf on this line and another burst on the Llanymynech line near Welsh Frankton on 5 February 1936 was not repaired; both lines were completely abandoned in 1944.

The first part of the Llanymynech branch is now dry in the neighbourhood of Welsh Frankton, but it contains water again after passing the site of the former Keeper's Bridge, near Rednal; it is piped under the A5 road at Queen's Head; and is piped again at Waen Wen and in the neighbourhood of Pant.

Welsh Frankton was the place which saw the last days and the final destruction of the famous packet boat *Duchess-Countess*. Its unusual name was due to the fact that a nephew of the last Duke of Bridgewater, and owner of the Donnington Wood Canal in East Shropshire, was created Duke of Stafford. When he married Elizabeth, the Countess of Sutherland in her own right, she became a Duchess as well as a Countess.

This passenger boat plied daily between Stockton Quay and Manchester for nearly 50 years. The trips started at 6 a.m. and finished at 7 p.m. The *Duchess-Countess* was manned by a crew of three - the captain, mate and 'jockey'. Although only of 6 ft. beam, her length allowed her to carry 30 passengers and provide for their refreshment. Drawn by relays of four horses, she travelled at six miles an hour.

Boats travelling outwards from Manchester had the right of way over those approaching the city, but the *Duchess-Countess,* the pride of the canal, had the right of way in either direction. Any boat disputing this right of way was summarily dealt with, for at her bow there was a large S-shaped knife, which cut through its opponent's tow rope in a most cavalier fashion!

Passengers became fewer as the 'railway age' progressed; and at last this proud old aristocrat of the canals was reduced to the ignominy of carrying goods, cattle and poultry, and bringing back fustian. Her daily trip was finally abandoned in 1915. She was tied up for a time at Stockton Quay, and then was give a fitting burial when she was taken to Runcorn and submerged with some other boats in the Big Pool.

Strangely enough this was not the end. After being submerged for 18 years, the *Duchess-Countess* was refloated and repaired in 1934, when a retired Warrington man refitted her and, with two friends, set out to explore the Ellesmere and neighbouring canals. One of these friends, a Mr. Mackie, eventually became the boat's owner and brought her to a pound between two of the locks at Welsh Frankton. Here he used her as a summer house-boat. Then the boat began to leak badly. It was wartime, and labour and materials were scarce. The *Duchess-Countess* was dragged out from the water and 'beached' near Nicholas Bridge, not far from the village. Finally Mr. Mackie decided to sell her. The British Waterways Museum curator inspected the boat, but decided that with so little of the original wood left, and that in so rotten a state, it was not worth restoring the packet; so it was eventually sold to a local farmer and broken up in 1956.

CHAPTER 6

INDUSTRIES SERVED BY THE ELLESMERE CANAL
1. COAL MINING

The Chirk Coalfield

At Black Park, just north of Chirk, coal has been mined since the reign of Elizabeth I. Small streams ran down steep valleys, and as coal seams reached the surface here and there, small scale opencast mining was carried out.

Later, shafts were sunk to reach the coal; but the seepage of water led to difficulties, as steam-operated pumps had not been invented. The method of drainage used was to dig tunnels - known as 'adits' - from the pit bottom; these sloped downwards and emerged at the surface at an even lower level. At the early Black Park colliery workings such an adit emptied its drainage water into the Billy Brook, just before this enters the River Dee (its exit can still be seen), and a large scale plan still exists showing the whole of the mine's adit system of drainage.

Close to small spoil heaps at these early Black Park workings is a row of houses named 'High Barracks', and nearby another row called 'Low Barracks'; these were probably miners' houses. The course of an old tramway can still be traced running to the Holyhead Road.

It was not until 1805 that more modern methods were introduced, when T.E. Ward leased the Black Park Colliery from the Chirk Castle estates. Between 1805 and 1825 Ward is said to have spent £20,000 on developing the mines and employed some 300 men.

A tramway ran from these later collieries under the Holyhead Road and finished alongside a dock running from the Ellesmere Canal. Facilities were provided for despatching coal by road at the 'Top Wharf' and by canal at the 'Lower Wharf'. The entrance to the dock was at the end of the

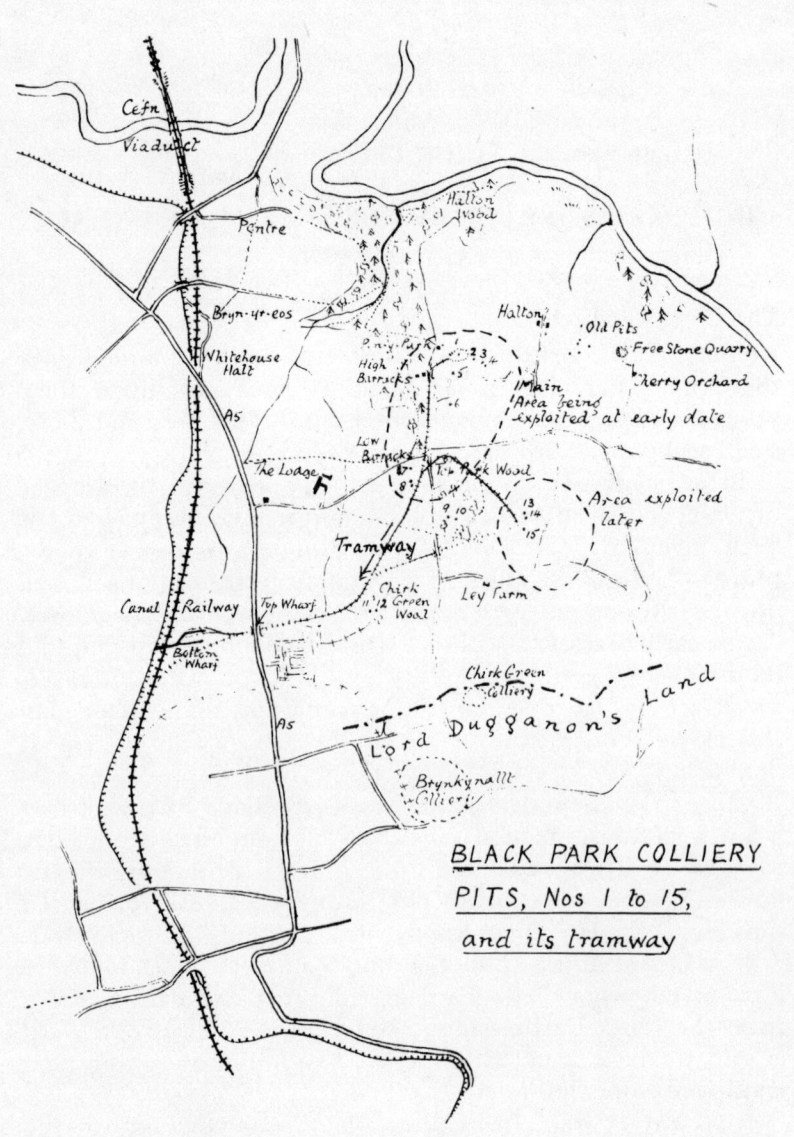

Cefn
Viaduct
Pentre
Bryn-yr-eos
Whitehouse
Halt
A5
High
Barracks
Low
Barracks
The Lodge
Tramway
Canal Railway   Top Wharf
Belton
Wharf
A5

Hilton Wood
Halton
Old Pits
Free Stone Quarry
Cherry Orchard
2 3 4
5
6
Main
Area being
exploited at early date
7
8
9 10
13
14
15
Area exploited
later
Chirk
Green
Wood
11 12
Ley Farm

Chirk Green
Colliery
Lord Dugganon's Land

Brynkynallt
Colliery

Black Park Wood

BLACK PARK COLLIERY
PITS, Nos 1 to 15,
and its tramway

wooded embankment on the towpath side of the deep
cutting after the Chirk Tunnel. Originally, this entrance was
spanned by a small bridge carrying the towpath. The canal's
dock arm then passed under a railway bridge before branching
into two arms, shaped like the letter Y. Here terminated the
horse-drawn tramway from the colliery. Later it was replaced
by a standard-gauge railway line. In the early 1950s the dock
and the underside of the railway bridge were filled in, making
the continuous embankment which is all that can now be seen.

As we approach Chirk we come to the early, small colliery
site at Chirk Green, and close to the A5 road the site of
Lord Dungannon's Brynkynalt Colliery which is a much larger
affair. Its huge spoil heap has been removed along with the
railway connecting the mines to the railway close by the canal.

South and west of the Chirk Aqueduct there were more
coalmines, all of them quite small and now extinct. They
were Lower Chirk Bank, Chirk Bank, Trehowell, Quinta,
Preesgwyne and Moreton Collieries. Most of them were
connected to the canal, or later to the railway, by tramways.
Moreton Colliery had the main railway line running through
it, and was also connected to the canal by a short, straight
tramway passing close by Moreton Hall Girls' School and
ending on an embankment where the canal passes under the
Holyhead Road. As a narrow dock from the canal runs past
the foot of this embankment coal was probably shot into
narrow boats down a chute.* On the other side of the road
bridge a wide wharf by the canal narrows down and joins the
main road, so that, as at the Black Park Colliery shipment
point, coal and other goods could be loaded or unloaded to
go by the canal or by the Holyhead Road.

In the direction of Chirk a high concrete bridge could be
seen spanning the road; this carried the colliery railway coming
from the Ifton Colliery to join up with the G.W.R. main
railway line (this bridge was demolished during 1971).

In the course of time the small collieries in the neighbourhood closed down, followed by the larger Brynkynalt in
1928 and Black Park in 1952, until finally all work was
concentrated in one pit, the Ifton Pit, close by the village of
St. Martins. This was modernised and employed nearly one

*This dock has now been filled in.

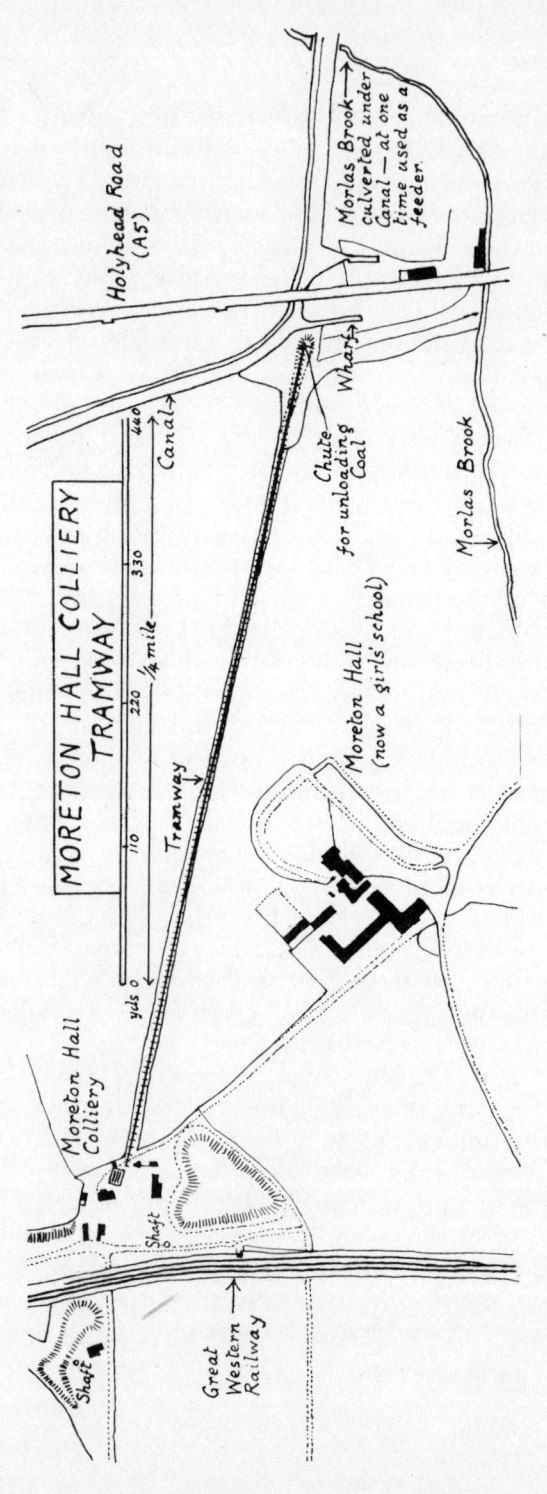

MORETON HALL COLLIERY
TRAMWAY

Holyhead Road (A5)

Canal

yds 0   110   220   330   440

¼ mile

Tramway

Moreton Hall Colliery

Great Western Railway

Shaft

Shaft

Moreton Hall
(now a girls' school)

Chute for unloading Coal

Wharf

Morlas Brook

Morlas Brook culverted under Canal — at one time used as a feeder.

thousand men, most of whom lived in St. Martins. Finally, even this colliery was closed on 25 November 1968, and today the long history of coal mining in the Chirk area has come to a close.

The Morda Coalfield

This was extensively worked during the 18th and 19th centuries. Situated just south of Oswestry it was the flourishing centre of a number of industries.

The 'Rough', near Sweeney Mountain, is studded over with the remains of 'bell-pit spoil heaps'. We know that industrialists began mining at the western end of the coalfield well before 1800, for, when the National Loan for combating Napoleon was raised in 1798, 140 colliers from the Llwyny-maen Colliery contributed £4 0s. 6d., and 70 colliers from the Trefarclwydd Colliery £2 14s. 6d. Many more pits were opened in the 19th century; and such associated industries as the raising of iron ore, and of clay and fireclay for pottery and brickmaking, were started.

Almost as soon as the canal was opened in this area in 1799, three small collieries unsuccessfully applied for permission to construct a tramway, some three miles long, to connect their pits with the canal. Another later attempt was successful, the tramway opening in 1813.

Tracking down the course of the old Colliery Tramway

Field Work

The only available information was the following paragraph from a pamphlet entitled 'The Morda Industries',

> This tramway crossed the fields to Nant-y-caws, and after running up the valley for some 200 yards, the track descended again and ran across the fields to the Welshpool road at Pwll-y-cwrw, going thence to Gronwen Wharf at Redwith - the latter built especially for the coal traffic and named after the colliery.

At the Morda crossroads just south of Oswestry our first enquiry set us immediately on the track of the old tramway leading from the site of the Drill Colliery (of which nothing now remains). Here it was quite easy to track the tramway

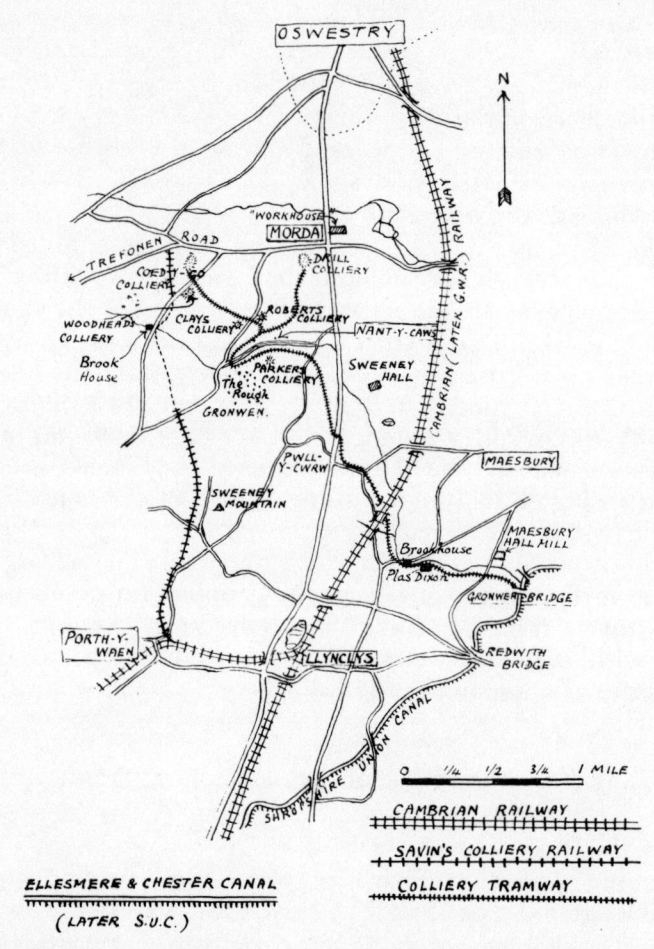

OSWESTRY

N

TREFONEN ROAD

"WORKHOUSE"
MORDA

MILL COLLIERY

COEDY-GO
COLLIERY

ROBERTS
COLLIERY

WOODHEADS
COLLIERY

CLAYS COLLIERY

NANT-Y-CAWS

Brook
House

PARKERS
COLLIERY

The
Rough

SWEENEY
HALL

GRONWEN.

CAMBRIAN (LATER G.W.R.) RAILWAY

PWLL-Y-CWRW

MAESBURY

SWEENEY
MOUNTAIN

MAESBURY
HALL HILL

Brookhouse

Plas Dixon

GRONWEN BRIDGE

PORTH-Y-WAEN

LLYNCLYS

REDWITH
BRIDGE

SHROPSHIRE UNION CANAL

0   1/4   1/2   3/4   1 MILE

CAMBRIAN RAILWAY

SAVIN'S COLLIERY RAILWAY

COLLIERY TRAMWAY

ELLESMERE & CHESTER CANAL

(LATER S.U.C.)

THE SWEENEY COLLIERY TRAMWAY (AND SAVIN'S RAILWAY)

course southwards as a wide, shallow depression. The track continued along what is now a short lane bordered by bushes, and then across another field to a stile. In the next field it veered southwestwards as it made a gradual descent to the stream flowing through the hamlet of Nant-y-caws, following the stream almost to a road junction before crossing and doubling back along the other side. The approach to the stream was marked by another depression, and one or two stone sleepers blocks were found in the stream.

Following the tramway's general direction, we picked up definite indications again where the course reached a country road. Here it curved round to run east of south, going through a spinney, which it left through an archway made of stone blocks 4 ft. 6 in. wide, with a headroom of possibly 5 ft. though it was now almost blocked by soil.

In the next field the depression then changed to a slight embankment. The main Oswestry-Welshpool road and Sweeney Hall were quite near on our left, and the tramway route gradually approached the road as we continued diagonally across the field. There were no indications of what happened next, although we were only a short distance from the side road marked Pwll-y-cwrw. However, at a later date, I was able to examine the Sweeney Hall estate maps which showed the tramway; and found that on reaching the road it crossed it at right angles, and then continued southwards some hundred yards before entering a spinney at the junction of the main and side roads. It came out of this spinney to run along the side road, and at the next road junction ran across a field in a southeasterly direction to penetrate the old Cambrian Railway embankment. Imagine our delight when we found, just beyond the embankment, almost 100 stone sleeper blocks, each with a central hole, and arranged in two rows - this was proof positive! The blocks were overgrown by grass, so we cleared a number of them and whitened them slightly with some of the chalky stones lying around, so that they would show up more clearly when photographed.

The blocks were roughly cubical, appearing approximately 1 ft. square at the surface of the ground. As the course of the tramway curved round to penetrate the embankment their arrangement was staggered. The distance between the holes in the successive blocks was 4 ft. 6 in. on the average, and the distance measured at right angles to the lines of blocks was 3 ft. 1 in. The rails used must have been about 4 ft. 6 in. long, held together by driving a flat headed iron spike into a wooden plug which occupied the hole in the sleeper block. How lucky we were to find these blocks in their original positions after 150 years!

We now were only three quarters of a mile from Redwith Bridge over the Ellesmere Canal, but we failed in our efforts to follow the tramway from here, nor could we find definite signs of a terminus at the bridge itself. However, later examination of maps showed that the next bridge was called 'Gronwen Bridge'; and although it was only an accommodation bridge with no road running to it, it was quite close to Redwith Bridge where three roads met. So we set out again to find out if the 'Gronwen Wharf' was situated here. There was a triangular inlet hard by the bridge which may have been the site of the coal wharf. We walked along a wide grass track leading in the general direction in which the tramway might have been expected to take, and crossing a road came to a meadow which was in the process of being ploughed up. Threequarters of the field had already been ploughed, but what luck! - on the edge of this portion there were nine stone sleeper blocks which had just been removed by the ploughman. These, and the fact that the soil was darker along the expected line of the tramway, provided us with solid evidence; and this was reinforced when we crossed into the next field and found two pairs of sleeper blocks in their original positions close to the Sweeney Brook. Others had come to rest in the bed of the brook. From here we were able to trace the short part which remained, and so completed our investigations.

Documentary Evidence

So far it had all been field work, but I was fortunate enough to get legal documents, letters and maps from the Sweeney Hall estate papers which provided definite documentary evidence - also the first edition of the 1″ Ordnance Survey map, published in the 1830s, showing the northern part of the tramway veering off to the northeast to end at the Coed-y-go Colliery. The owner of Sweeney Hall, Thomas Netherton Parker, had a shaft, 269 ft. deep, sunk in a field adjacent to the 'Rough'; but in 1808 Messrs. Samuel Leach, Richard Croxon, John Croxon and Edward Croxon formed the 'Sweeney Company' for mining coal in the Sweeney township. They approached various landowners in the area to obtain leases, and took over several pits, including that of Mr. Parker.

It seems that the coal obtained from Mr. Parker's Colliery was poor, both in quality and quantity; and in 1812 the Croxons endorsed the lease to the effect that, in return for the right of ceasing to work Parker's Colliery at any time, and of being able to surrender the lease on six months notice after 25 March 1813 if they wished, they, in their turn, would pay Mr. Parker a yearly minimum sum of £300 as long as the lease was in existence, and *by 25th March 1813 would complete a railway* [i.e. a tramway] *from the said colliery to the canal,* which Mr. Parker should be at liberty to use if the the lease was surrendered.

In a later complaint against the Croxons Mr. Parker stated,

they carried the railway to a distant coalworks, and never brought it to, nor used it for, Mr. Parker's coals [actually it passed within 100 yards of Parker's Colliery]; on the contrary, upon the same day that they endorsed the lease to pay Mr. Parker at least £300 a year, they also signed a notice to surrender the lease in six months.

This sharp practice led to Mr. Parker bringing a legal action against the Croxons; but although he won his case he was only awarded nominal damages, making it more of a moral victory than a financial one.

The canal tramway was extended to finish at the Coed-y-go Colliery of Messrs. T. & J. Savin, the owners in the 1860s. They decided to build a private standard-gauge railway from their colliery to the junction at Llynclys with the Welsh railways then being built. Most of its course can still be followed quite easily.

CHAPTER 7

INDUSTRIES SERVED BY THE ELLESMERE CANAL
2. LIMESTONE & LIME

The Ellesmere canal ran through some marshy and badly drained country, and in the 1805 *Report* we find the statement,

> It is from fuel and manure for agricultural purposes that its most important and permanent revenue must be looked for.

Whenever the word 'manure' is used in these early reports it stands for 'lime'. Boggy land tends to develop an acid reaction unfavourable for the growth of plants, and often it is of a heavy, clayey nature. Both the acidity and the stickiness of the soil are removed by repeated additions of lime.

Thus, almost as soon as work on digging the canal started, priority was given to the branch leading from Welsh Frankton to the limestone rocks at Llanymynech. It was opened in 1797. These rocks occur as high inland cliffs alongside the Oswestry-Welshpool road, from Llynclys Hill by Pant to Llanymynech. There are further rocks of a similar nature nearby at Porthywaen, Nantmawr and Llanyblodwel.

The rock was of good quality for making lime, but was at a great height compared with the canal, so that ways and means had to be developed to get the quarried limestone down to the level of the canal. At the Llanymynech quarries are pairs of very thick limestone walls a few yards apart at the head of long, even slopes; in 1950 these were much overgrown with bushes, brambles and other plant growth. It seems likely that these walls may have supported the large drums on which chain was wound in order to lower trucks of quarried limestone down an incline, and haul up the empties. One such drum still stands behind a shop in Pant. It consists of a thick, wooden spindle supporting several iron wheels, and across the rims of these wheels there are short wooden

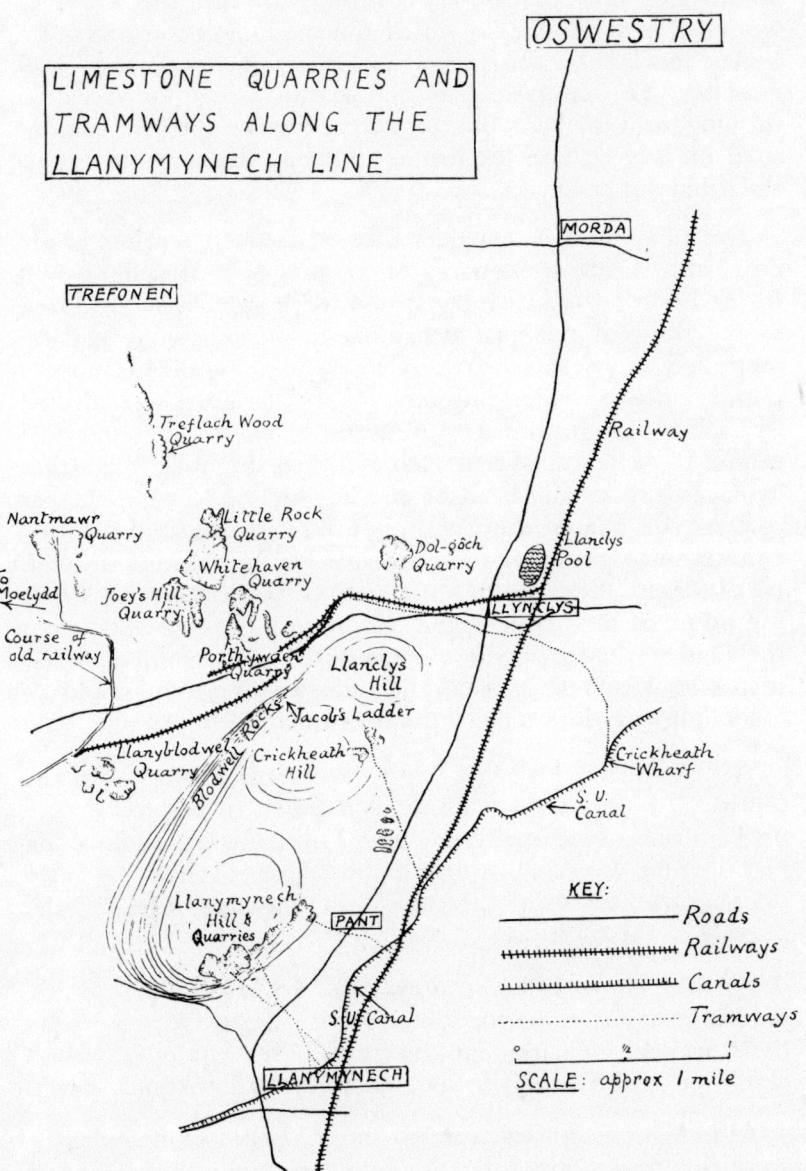

LIMESTONE QUARRIES AND
TRAMWAYS ALONG THE
LLANYMYNECH LINE

OSWESTRY

MORDA

TREFONEN

Treflach Wood
Quarry

Railway

Nantmawr
Quarry

Little Rock
Quarry

Dol-gôch
Quarry

Llanclys
Pool

To
Moelydd

Whitehaven
Quarry

LLYNCLYS

Joey's Hill
Quarry

Course of
old railway

Porthywaen
Quarry

Llanclys
Hill

Jacob's Ladder

Crickheath
Wharf

Llanyblodwel
Quarry

Crickheath
Hill

S.U.
Canal

Llanymynech
Hill &
Quarries

PANT

KEY:

———————— Roads

+++++++++++++++ Railways

······················ Canals

- - - - - - - - - Tramways

S.U. Canal

LLANYMYNECH

SCALE: approx 1 mile

boards forming the outer covering; around the drum is wound a considerable length of the original chain; parts of a brake mechanism operating on the right outer rim still remain.   The course of an old tramway can be detected running from the Pant Quarry, across the Oswestry-Welshpool road on a level with the drum, and then down an incline to the dried out canal.

The Llanymynech Quarries were extensively worked in the past; and inside the quarry there is a pair of walls which formerly supported a haulage drum, with an incline excavated in the floor of the quarry leading to an enormous, square-sectioned tunnel, some 30 ft. by 30 ft., piercing the hillside - an impressive work when one remembers that holes were drilled by hand and gunpowder used for blasting.   Beyond this tunnel there was a level stretch and then the walls of another haulage drum at the head of another incline.   From another part of the quarry there was a second incline, and the two converged to go under the Oswestry-Welshpool road through two tunnels (these are unnoticeable from road level).   From the point of their convergence a common tramway led across the field to the canal where docks had been dug and embankments constructed, so that the quarried limestone could be loaded directly into narrow boats or down a chute.

A little nearer Llynclys there were further quarries in the hillside from which a tramway led down to the canal close by Pant railway station, going under the railway and finishing just beyond the canal bridge at the adjacent canal. An extra opening in the wall of the canal bridge was provided for the passage of the tramway.

Further along still a tramway led from the Porthywaen limestone quarries to the canal at Crickheath Wharf, where there was an embankment almost certainly equipped with a chute in former days, and a wharf at towpath level.

Although we can learn much about the limestone industry from this neighbourhood it is a long time since any quarrying was carried out here; but one of the quarries formerly connected with the Ellesmere Canal was fully operative in 1954.   This was the Pen-y-graig Quarry at Vroncysyllte, quite

close to the Pontcysyllte Aqueduct. Like those in the region
of Llanymynech, this quarry was at a considerable height
above the canal, and on its way down the tramway first
descended an incline, and then went on a level stretch where
horse-traction was used before descending the second and
third inclines to the level of the Holyhead road. Just across
the road were six limekilns with their tops at road level, and
the bottom exits immediately adjacent to the Ellesmere Canal.
The tramway branched into two on reaching the road, one
branch crossing the road on a level; and in 1954 one could
still experience the extraordinary sight of two men with red
flags holding up the traffic on this A5 road as the horse and
its two trucks of quarried limestone crossed over - this would
hardly be permitted today! In former days a second branch
of the tramway descended by a tunnel under the road to a
fair-sized triangular dock where the limestone was loaded on
to narrow boats - by 1954 this had been filled in.

A system of pipes connected to an air-compressor covered
the quarry area, and pneumatic drills were used to drill the
holes for the explosive used in blasting. After the fall of the
rock, pieces of a suitable size were sorted out and loaded on
to small wooden trucks which were open on one side. Then
the pair of loaded trucks began their slow descent of the
first incline; soon a pair of empty trucks could be seen
ascending, connected to the same endless hawser; the track
doubled where it formed a loop and here the two pairs of
trucks were able to pass. At the bottom of the first incline
there was a side quarry being worked, and a horse was
harnessed to the trucks to pull them along a level stretch
under a picturesque, high bridge and through a rock cutting
to the large haulage drum at the head of the second incline.
This was about the same size as the drum at Pant, and was
suspended between two limestone walls; but it differed in
using wire hawser in place of chain, in having the brake
acting centrally, and in being covered by a corrugated iron
shelter. However, in the woods lower down was a drum
skeleton identical with that at Pant, and the quarry workers
said that those in use had been brought here from the Glyn
Ceiriog slate quarries when they closed down.

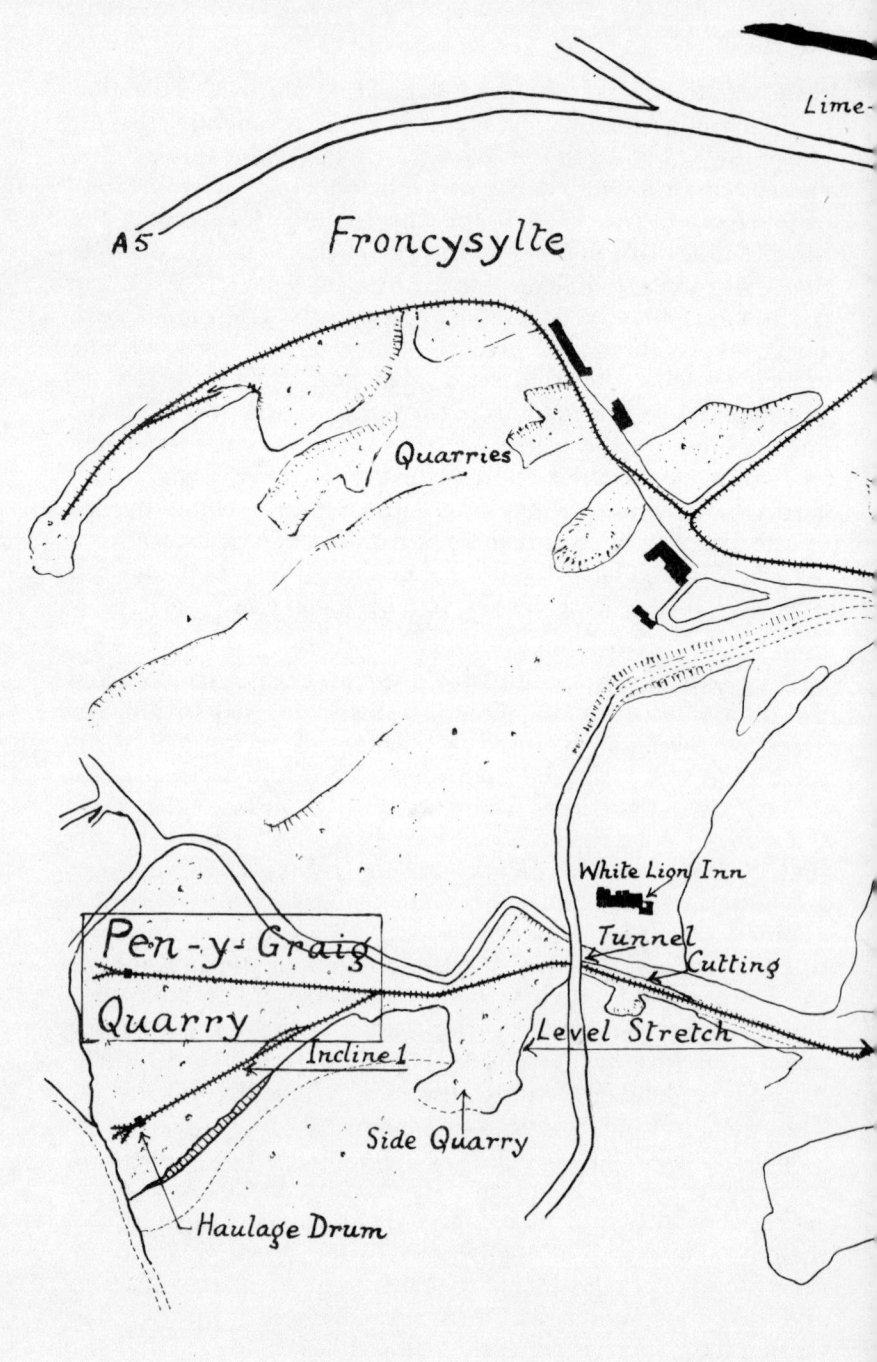

Lime—

A5   Froncysylte

Quarries

White Lion Inn

Pen-y-Graig
Quarry

Tunnel
Cutting

Incline 1

Level Stretch

Side Quarry

Haulage Drum

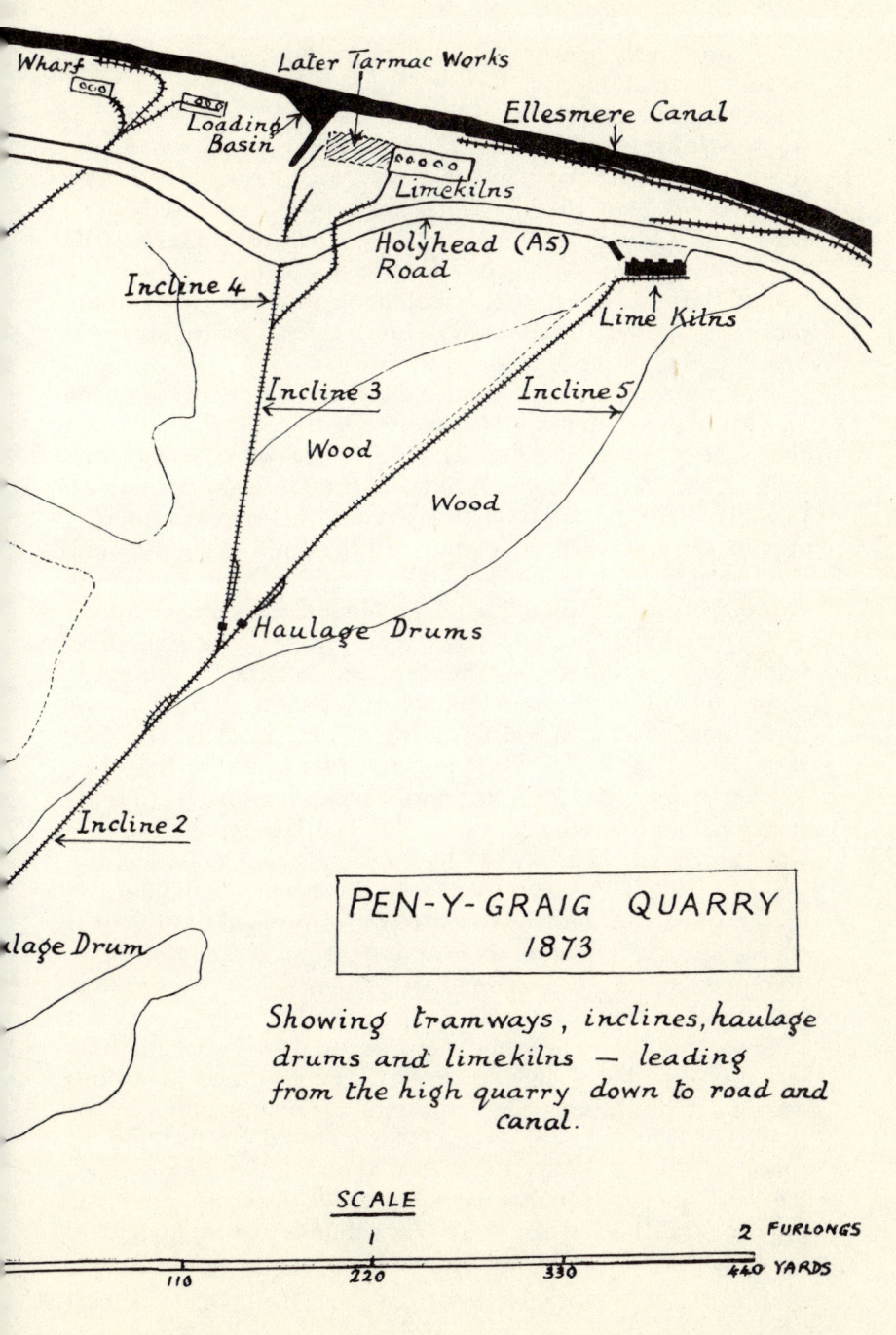

Wharf

Later Tarmac Works

Loading
Basin

Ellesmere Canal

Limekilns

Holyhead (A5)
Road

Incline 4

Lime Kilns

Incline 3

Incline 5

Wood

Wood

Haulage Drums

Incline 2

...lage Drum

PEN-Y-GRAIG QUARRY
1873

Showing tramways, inclines, haulage
drums and limekilns — leading
from the high quarry down to road and
canal.

SCALE

1

2 FURLONGS

110   220   330   440 YARDS

As previously mentioned a third incline brought the load down to road level. But in 1954, what happened next differed from the events of the early days because by then no limestone was dispatched either by road or canal, the tunnel under the road and the canal loading dock had been blocked up, and the limekilns were no longer used. The limestone was still taken across the road at this time; but the trucks were then placed on a tipping platform, and the stone tipped into a very noisy crushing plant, after which the pieces were graded. This was because tarmac was being made here by coating the graded stone with tar.

Not many years later the quarry closed down owing to the lack of skilled labour. The tarmac works carried on for a time using stone quarried at the Nantmawr quarries some miles away, but finally closed also. In any case, holding up the traffic on the A5 road today would be a great nuisance, and in the last year or so the road itself has been widened, straightened and modernised just here, so that today the entrance to the third incline of the old quarry is quite hidden.

Further limestone quarries connected with the Ellesmere Canal were situated on the far side of the Pontcysyllte Aqueduct, quite near to Llangollen. We first come to the fairly small Trevor Wood Quarries, not far from Trevor Hall, then the main Trevor Quarries, and finally to the Eglwyseg Rocks, rising to 1,000 ft. and having impressive, sloping strata visible for miles around. The last quarry to close here was the Trevor Quarry. It had a very steep incline with a gradient of 1 in 5 leading down to the canal. At the bottom of the slope the tramway used to cross the road to unload at the canal; and on more than one occasion the chain broke, precipitating the truck loaded with limestone across the road and almost across the canal!

From this quarry another tramway led westwards, climbing steadily up the Eglwyseg Rocks, going under a bridge carrying a very minor road and finally reaching such a height that the 1,000 ft. conical hill surmounted by the ancient ruins of Castell Dinas Brân just across the valley seemed hardly higher. It must have been awe-inspiring quarrying limestone up here when there was a thunderstorm, high wind or snow; but the tramway undoubtedly ran along this route, as in places the wooden sleepers still project from the narrow ledge.

The quality of the limestone obtained at these quarries was suitable for using as a flux in iron smelting. The charge added to the blast furnace consists of iron ore, coke and limestone, and the purpose of the limestone is to combine with the impurities present to form a fusible slag which floats on the molten iron at the bottom of the furnace, and is run off at intervals. This allows the furnace to be worked continuously over a period of years.

A certain amount was taken by a very circuitous route: over the Pontcysyllte Aqueduct, through Chirk, Ellesmere, and Whitchurch to Nantwich, where it went down the Birmingham and Liverpool Canal as far as Norbury Junction, and then along the Newport Canal to the East Shropshire Blast Furnaces. Other cargoes went as far as Birmingham and other Midland towns.

Although a certain amount of limestone was used in towpath construction, in iron smelting, for the exteriors of limekilns, and for making tarmac, the bulk of it was used in the making of lime. To convert limestone into lime it has to be heated strongly. If the purity of the lime was unimportant it could be mixed with coal and heated in a kiln; if a purer lime was wanted a fire could be maintained at the bottom of the kiln, and the kiln was then filled with limestone only. Today lime is made by a continuous process, the heat being produced by gas firing. In the early days of the canal it was always made in kilns; these were often built in blocks of two to six. There is a block of two kilns at Colemere, where the canal is at a higher level than the mere so that the top of the kilns is level with the canal, making for easy loading. At Hampton Bank there is a wharf by the bridge where limestone was unloaded and taken to the top of the 'Bank' to be loaded into the block of three kilns. Weston Lullingfields, the actual terminus on the unfinished Shrewsbury line, was equipped to supply the surrounding country with lime, and possessed a block of four limekilns; while the other unfinished branch line which went from the main line of the canal at Whixall Moss and stopped just beyond Edstaston instead of Prees, had a block of five kilns arranged against a bank in a shallow curve at Quina Brook, adjacent to the Wem-Whitchurch road. To complete the series there is a block of six kilns at Vroncysyllte which used to receive limestone from the Pen-y-graig Quarries in the days when the quarry and the kilns were both active.

Remains of the kilns mentioned can still be seen, although several now serve to house farm implements or garage a car, and at Quina Brook there is such a growth of bushes and trees that a close search must be made to discover the entrances to the kilns. At the top of the incline at Trevor there is quite a well preserved block of three kilns on one side, whilst a similar block of three on the other side is so broken down that it shows the construction of the kilns very well. Kilns were nearly always built near the limestone quarries themselves; there are five just above the canal at Pant where the incline ends, and several along the high level portion connecting Pant quarries with those at Llanymynech, while a very long, steep ramp at Llanymynech was built up from the meadow to end at the top of a really gigantic kiln close to the canal. An early type of continuous kiln can be seen nearby; it is a long oval in shape with entrances all round leading to an interior which runs continuously around a long central wall. In use, limestone and coal were added opposite two or three of the entrances, and 'burning' started, being aided by flues leading to a tall chimney outside. As the burning spread so more limestone and coal were added, gradually working around the kilns of the whole oval building. Well before the circuit was completed the original burning had ceased, the lime formed had cooled and had been unloaded, and then fresh charges of limestone and coal were added.

Not all the limekilns now remain, but some of them were shown on the large scale Ordnance Survey maps. Thus a block of two kilns is marked adjacent to Maestermyn Bridge where the Oswestry-Ellesmere road passes over the canal; not a stone remains today, but its former existence is proved by the map and a bill heading of the Maestermyn, Quina Brook and Ellesmere Lime Company.

CHAPTER 8

INDUSTRIES SERVED BY THE ELLESMERE CANAL
3. SLATE & SLATE-SLAB

The Oernant Quarry Tramway

In the original plans of both the 'Western Line' and the 'Eastern Line', a branch of the canal was included to go along the Vale of Llangollen and terminate as close as possible to the slate and slate-slab quarries just beyond the bend in the Horseshoe Pass at Oernant (sometimes spelt Irenant). Like the limestone quarries these were situated high above the canal. To get the quarried material down to the canal involved the building of another tramway.

In 1852 a tramway, five miles long, was built by the well known engineer, Henry Dennis, who was only 27 years old at the time. It connected the Oernant Quarry with the Ellesmere Canal at Pentre'r-felin - this lies beyond Llangollen not far from the Horseshoe Weir where the canal begins. In 1948 derelict buildings, marked on an old, large scale Ordnance Survey map as the 'Pentre'r-felin Slab and Slate Works' were still to be seen. A few years later the same buildings had been acquired by another firm and were being used for the grinding and grading of silica; later still it was taken over by the Deeside Sheet Metal Company. The original work done here had been transferred to the Slate-Slab Quarries at Oernant.

There is no longer a tramway for it is unnecessary now there is quite a good road over the Horseshoe Pass; but we wanted to discover the course of the old tramway. A large scale Ordnance Survey map of 1873 shows the part of it adjacent to the canal. Here the abutments of a small bridge (probably a 'swing-bridge' type) indicate the spot where the tramway left the works and crossed the canal. Then it ran up a private drive (now obliterated by an embankment) and

83

crossed low-lying land on an embankment 105 yd. long and 30 ft. high, the Eglwyseg River (a mere stream) passing through a high, central archway faced with stone blocks; two further archways penetrated the bank on either side of this opening, that on the left carrying a millstream formerly supplying power to the Pentre'r-felin Corn Mill on the far side of the A452 road.

Soon after leaving the embankment the tramway crossed the road and ran alongside it through the lovely Valle Crucis valley. It then altered its direction and made a bee-line for a mountain which completely blocked its path. The tramway must next have climbed the mountain which is about 400 ft. high, with a gradient approaching 1:1 in places. It appeared far too steep to have had trucks running on rails, and one surmises that sledges must have been used. There were hollows flanked by slates, arranged 5 ft. 6 in. apart; in one of these was a pulley wheel and some wire hawser.

About 200 ft. up one reaches a well-built, slate-faced embankment on each side of the incline - probably supports for a former haulage drum. It is possible that the incline was surfaced with slate, as in 1957 we found four 2 ft. square slates spiked to the ground about 3 ft. apart - two slates on one side of the slope and two on the other.

After another 200 ft. we reached the point where the tramway course ran to the right on a level, skirting round the head of a valley and finishing up at the Oernant Quarry.

The Glyn Valley Tramway

Slate had also been quarried near Glynceiriog since the 1500s, although on a very small scale because the quarries were too far from the nearest distribution centre for larger scale working to be possible. They were six miles up the valley of the River Ceiriog, and those six miles were a veritable 'thorn in the flesh' for those industrialists who tried hard to improve the situation.

The story of their attempts is long and involved. Only after 16 years' continuous struggle did a horse-drawn tramway see the light of day.

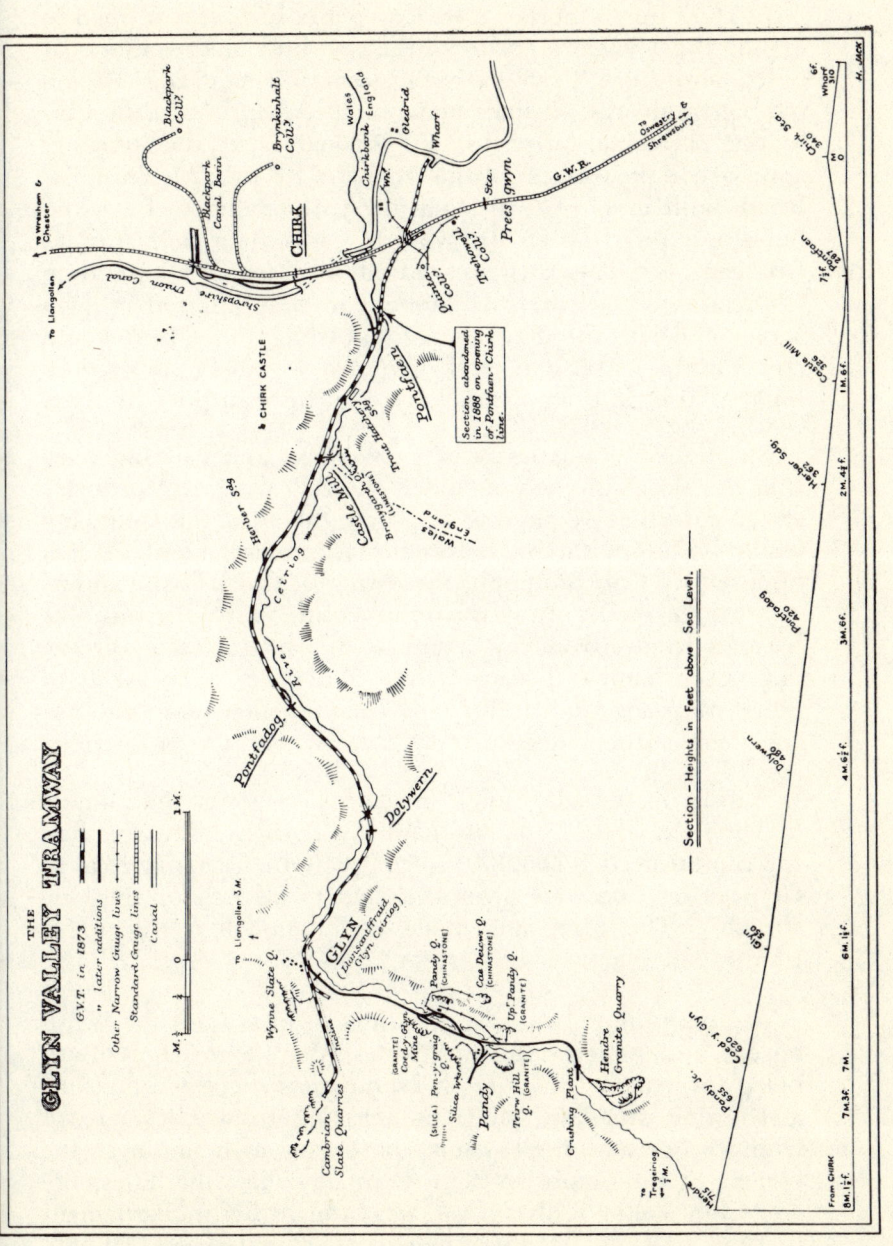

THE GLYN VALLEY TRAMWAY

GVT. in 1873 ━━━━━━━
„ later additions ━━━━━━━
Other Narrow Gauge lines ━━━━━━━
Standard Gauge lines ═══════

Canal ═══════

M. ½ 0 1 M.

To Wrexham & Chester ←

Blackpark Coll?
Blackpark Canal Basin
Brynkinalt Coll?

To Llangollen

Shropshire Union Canal

Ellesmere Canal

CHIRK

Wales
England
Chirkbank
Oldr'd.
Wharf
Wh.
Wharf
Phoenix Coll?
Wynnstay Coll?
Sta.
Preesgwyn

G.W.R.

To Oswestry & Shrewsbury →

♦ CHIRK CASTLE

Pontfaen

Section abandoned in 1888 on opening of Pontfaen-Chirk line.

Harter S.H9

Castle Mill

Bridge to Ty'n-y-Wern (England)
Tan-y-fron
Wales England

River Ceiriog

Pontfadog

Dolywern

To Llangollen 3M.

Wynne Slate Q.

Cambrian Slate Quarries

Pen-y-graig
(SLATE)
Sluice House!

Pandy

Quinta Coll?

GLYN (Llansantffraid Glyn Ceiriog)

Pandy Q. (GRANITE)
Cae Deicws Q. (GRANITE)
Up? Pandy Q. (GRANITE)

Pen-y-graig Candy Glyn Mine (GRANITE)

Trew. Hill Q.

Crushing Plant

Hendre Granite Quarry

To Tregeiriog 7 M.

─── Section – Heights in Feet above Sea Level. ───

From CHIRK

8 M.½f.
S'h.
7 M.½f.
7 M.
Glyn
Good
650
6 M.½f.
611
5 M.
575
Pandy 4M.
4 M.6f.
Pontfadog
490
3 M.6f.
420
2 M.4f.
Hendre Sidg.
385
Castle Mill
365
1 M.6f.
Pontfaen
340
Chirk Sta.
290
Wharf
264

H. Mock.

In 1857 the Cambrian Slate Company, Ltd., was formed to exploit the Glynceiriog slate for the first time on a commercial basis; and in a flush of enthusiasm it spent £22,000 on quarry tramways, inclines and buildings, optimistically estimating an annual output of 4,000 tons. Next, the company approached the trustees of the Wem and Bronygarth Turnpike Road, built in 1771, which ran down the valley as far as the limestone quarries at Bronygarth - less than half way to Glynceiriog. The trustees wanted to extend their road to Glynceiriog but had little money; so they entered into an agreement with the slate company in which the latter would pay for this extension, and in return would be allowed to build a tramway along its verge for the transport of slate.

So far, so good, but when producing the Parliamentary Bill, the slate company included the following extraordinary statement 'that if anyone opposed the idea the Company would withdraw the Bill before it reached Parliament.' It *was* opposed by Col. Biddulph, the owner of Chirk Castle and its estates. As the tramway was an urgent necessity the turnpike trustees tried introducing a similar Bill, but this was thrown out of Parliament because 'they had never been asked to unite railroads and turnpike roads together and did not consider it their duty to do so now for the first time.'

Acting on the adage that 'half a loaf is better than none,' in 1863 the Slate Company paid the Turnpike Trustees half the capital needed (£5,000) to complete the turnpike road to Glynceiriog, and were given the right to all tolls on this new stretch. The road was made wide enough to include a tramway at a later date.

At this time railways were springing up around the Welsh border and penetrating into Wales, the Cambrian Railway being formed in 1864. Local landowners suggested building a 13 mile standard gauge branch line from Ellesmere to Glynceiriog, and hopes must have run high amongst the owners of the Cambrian Slate Company when the 'Ellesmere and Glyn Valley Railway Act' was brought before Parliament in 1866. The cost of this scheme was estimated at £120,000, but as the money was not forth-coming it was dropped.

By this time the Slate Company was getting desperate, and in 1869 brought out an Act for an eight mile narrow-gauge tramway to run from Glynceiriog to the G.W.R. line halfway between Chirk and Preesgwyne Stations; here the tramway would divide, one part following the track of a pre-1835 tramway that had linked two small collieries at Upper Chirk Bank with a wharf and narrow boat basin on the Ellesmere Canal near to the 'New Inn' at Gledrid; the other going to exchange sidings with the G.W.R. line. The company hoped that once built the line could be rented or sold to the G.W.R. or the Cambrian Railway, or even to the canal company. However, the next year saw the introduction of the Tramway Act allowing tramways to be laid along roads in towns. The abandoned idea of running a tramway down the turnpike road to Chirk was instantly revived and, in August 1870, produced the 'Glyn Valley Tramway Act'. In it the tramway company agreed to pay the turnpike trustees an annual rent of £150.

Once again finance reared its ugly head. The Cambrian Slate Company felt it had already paid out enough, and local landowners were not keen to provide the money. In desperation the promoters approached the Shropshire Union Railways and Canal Company who agreed to provide half the necessary capital (£5,000) in return for control over constructional work and sole rights to work the line.

Building began at long last in June 1872. The gauge selected was unique amongst narrow gauge lines in Britain, namely 2 ft. 4¼ in., no better reason being given for this than that it was half the standard gauge. The track ran down the valley from Glynceiriog alongside the road, with a down gradient of 1 in 110, so that it could be gravity operated as far as Pontfaen. Here it crossed the river on its own bridge and almost immediately ascended a hill with a maximum gradient of 1 in 30, followed by a half mile level stretch, and a gentle gradient down to the canal.

The terminus at the canal consisted of a stone-edged wharf and a basin set at 45° to the canal which was just large enough to accommodate two narrow boats. It has been built to serve the Upper Chirk Bank coal pits some 50 years before but had fallen into disuse. A triangular reversing set of tracks and a few sidings were added. On the far side of the canal there is a row of houses and of stables which probably date from those days of horse traction.

Where the tramway crossed the G.W.R. line (lying in a cutting here) a spur of 250 yards ran parallel to the G.W.R. line to meet an exchange siding.

Gravity was used as the motive power on the journey from Glynceiriog to Pontfaen, but a horse was carried in the guard's van so that it could pull the 'tram' on the return journey! Financially the line was a failure, due to the fact that at Pontfaen the slate trucks had to be run into sidings and broken down into lots small enough for a horse to pull them up the 800 yards of steep incline.

For eight years the canal company continued to run the line, but at a total loss of £7,061. One reason for hanging on was the prospect of a new market in small hard blocks of stone (setts) which were being used in increasing quantity for urban street tramways. There was plenty of granite at Hendre, six miles beyond Glynceiriog, and in 1875 the Glynceiriog Granite Company was formed to produce these granite setts; an increase in the tramway traffic was confidently expected to result. However, their efforts to introduce steam traction at this time, and to re-route the line to Chirk, failed; and there was so much unpleasantness in the Board Room and with shareholders, that the canal company gave up its management of the line and sold all works and plant to the Glyn Valley Tramway Company in 1881.

The Glynceiriog Granite Company produced 10,000 tons of granite setts at its Hendre Quarries in the first year of operation of the new ownership of the tramway, and the latter showed a profit of £15. However, in the same year the Cambrian Slate Company went into liquidation and little slate was produced in the succeeding years; and after a few more years there was a decline in the granite traffic. The 'up-traffic' remained steady, taking coal and other goods up the valley, and a passenger service was run from 1874 to 1886.

The G.V.T. soon realised that the only way to make their line pay was to introduce steam-traction and re-route the track from Pontfaen. A Bill was introduced, called the 'Glyn Valley Tramways Act, 1885'; the conversion to steam traction began in 1887 and was completed in 1888. The track now crossed the road near the Chirk Fisheries and ran on the far side of the wall close by the road. It involved a quarter of a mile of cutting at the summit level of the climb up to Chirk G.W.R. Station. Here the G.V.T. had its own station just behind the G.W.R. station.

The realignment of the track cut out the portion which used to run from Pontfaen to the canal terminus at Gledrid; nevertheless the tramway did not lose its connection with the canal because lines were laid from its Chirk Station, extending for three quarters of a mile to make contact with the canal dock at the Black Park shipment point (see page 66). In 1906 the canal company built a siding, chute and wharf here where roadstone was tipped into narrow boats, and Henry Dennis ran a small pavement slab and street kerb making plant, the G.V.T. delivering quarry dust and ballast; coal from the Black Park Colliery was also loaded into canal boats at this point.

The introduction of locomotive traction improved the finances of the company, although it could never be said to be flourishing, but it certainly helped to develop the industries of the Glynceiriog Valley. The Hendre Quarry had two million tons of granite removed by the G.V.T., and in place of setts and kerb stones there were chippings, tarmacadam, railway ballast and stonedust. The slate quarries opened again about 1890, the Wynn and Cambrian quarries each producing about 2,000 tons of slates per year. Figures for 1913 showed traffic receipt percentages as follows:

Granite	50%
Coal and Coke	7%
Slate	6%
Passengers	18%

and the excess of income over expenditure for the year as £1,570.

The wars had their effect on the prosperity of the line, but it gradually became more of a liability as road haulage took over; and its end came on 6 July 1935 after 62 years of service, of which 47 years were in steam.

CHAPTER 9

INDUSTRIES SERVED BY THE ELLESMERE CANAL
4. FLOUR MILLING

The Morda Brook may look an insignificant water-course, but before the Ellesmere Canal was completed it was drawn upon to supply water for the canal as a temporary measure - the even smaller Morlas Brook was used too. In former times Morda Brook also supplied the power needed for working a number of water mills along its course. Today most of these have ceased to operate and in some cases the buildings have gone, the millponds have been drained: while in one case a former millpond now serves as an allotment.

A notable exception is the Maesbury Hall Mill of Messrs. A. & A. Peate, Ltd.. It has a lovely setting hard by the now derelict portion of the old Ellesmere Canal. The mill itself is a strictly utilitarian structure, and the modern additions which dominate the buildings have corrugated iron exteriors; but for all that, it is imposing in its size and proportions, and is a model of efficiency.

The best viewpoint is from the canal just by the bridge. A wide, funnel-shaped offshoot of the canal narrows down to a point from which it used to continue as a small channel just wide enough to accommodate a single narrow boat on its way to the Mill Wharf; the boat had to return stern first. Today the channel is filled in; but the view from the canal over the wider portion, framed on either side with trees, with meadows occupying the intervening space up to the Mill, and more trees forming the background, presents a most satisfying picture.

Built on the site of a former malt kiln, Maesbury Hall Mill has been a family concern of the Peates since 1862 when it was bought by the present owner's great-grandfather, Mr. Andrew Peate who operated it until his death in 1872.

His widow then let the mill for the next 15 years until her eldest son, Andrew, was old enough to take over in 1887. Her second son, Albert, joined Andrew in 1892, and their partnership continued until 1927 when Andrew retired. The previous managing director, Mr. Frank Peate, joined his father when his uncle died in 1931; and on the death of his father in 1941 took over the management of the mill himself. He died, 18 December 1970, and his son is carrying on.*

Originally the mill was operated by a waterwheel fed from the Morda Brook. Later, the wheel was replaced by a vertically-operated water-turbine, worked by a 24 ft. fall of water; it is now supplemented by electrical power. A few hundred yards to the north, at the hamlet of Newbridge, there are weirs and sluices which enable the miller to direct the water from the brook into a substantial millpond, and from thence by an artificial channel to the mill itself. After it has done its work of driving the water-turbine the water is led back to the Morda Brook by a further cut culverted under the canal. Thus a short length of the brook is temporarily cut off while the miller makes use of it.

A fire in 1911 did considerable damage, gutting the provender mill, warehouse and screen room; but this only proved a temporary check as they were all rebuilt before the year was out. The following year saw the addition of a new silo of 700 tons capacity; and a new warehouse was built eight years later.

Electrification of the mill took place in 1933, and soon afterwards the storage capacity was increased by extending the old silo and constructing a new one. Another improvement was the provision of a drier-house to deal with home grown wheat, as this all arrived at about the same time and in too great a quantity to be dealt with immediately. After a typical English summer it was often too damp for safe storage, and thus had to be dried and stored until such time as it could be milled.

NOTE. On 21 August 1971 a disastrous fire practically destroyed the mill. Flour milling is to be discontinued. Only animal feeding stuffs will be manufactured.

Grain is obtained from a radius of some 40 miles around the mill, but much of the grain used is imported from Canada via Liverpool. Many years ago the Ellesmere Canal provided the best means of transport between Maesbury and Liverpool; and when, in 1921, the canal owners ceased to do their own carrying, the Peates bought a fleet of eleven narrow boats from them, most of the boats being named after famous victories in British history, *Cressy, Aboukir,* etc.

Corn from Canada was landed at Liverpool, where the grain was transferred in bulk to 100 ton barges, and these took it across the Mersey estuary to Ellesmere Port. Here it was discharged into the large warehouses until the narrow boats came alongside to be loaded up. 2 cwt. sacks were then filled with the grain, and loaded into the boats until they contained their usual complement of about 20 tons.

The long journey to Maesbury by canal then began. Across the Wirral Peninsula to Chester; along the old Chester Canal as far as Hurleston Junction near Nantwich; then by the old Ellesmere Canal again, via Wrenbury, Whitchurch, Ellesmere, Welsh Frankton, Queen's Head and Aston Locks; and at last, after negotiating 41 locks, to Maesbury.

At the mill the sacks of grain were hoisted up from the boats, and emptied into the bulk stores. It took five days to get from Maesbury to Ellesmere Port and back, and one day for loading and another for unloading; that is about a week for the whole journey. When the Peates took over the boats they also took over the crews, paying them on tonnage at the rate of 2s. 10d. per ton. About 20 tons was carried per week by each boat, so that if nothing else was carried each boat would earn about £3 per week. However, it was usually arranged for empty boats to pick up other cargoes, such as road stone, sand, timber, etc., if they were needed. In this way earnings might reach £5 per week.

By the year 1930 practically the only people besides the Peates making commercial use of this part of the canal were the coal merchants Owen & Sons of Pant, Hydes of Welsh Frankton, and Edwards of Maesbury Marsh. The coal came from the Black Park Colliery's wharf near Chirk, and the Peates also obtained 20 tons per week for use in the mill.

With very little revenue coming in by way of tolls, the canal authorities so neglected the maintenance of the waterway that the canal began to silt up. When fully loaded the boats touched bottom in many places, making progress extremely slow and difficult, so that merchants had to lighten the loads carried until at last this method of transport became uneconomic. In 1932 the Peates stopped using boats and sold their fleet to the Leeds and Liverpool Canal Company and others.

During its more prosperous days the Shropshire Union Canal Company (as it was then called) had built warehouses and depots at Newtown, Welshpool, Berriew, Maesbury Marsh, Ellesmere and Whitchurch, all solid, substantial buildings, of which that at Maesbury Marsh was rented by the Peates (it was destroyed by fire on 23 April 1968). Stocks of grain, flour and many other goods were kept at these depots; and when the Shropshire Union Canal Company ceased carrying, the Peates sent boats to restock some of the depots occasionally.

When the boats owned by the Peates were in need of repair they were sent to Welsh Frankton (see page 61). The boat builder was Mr. Beech. He repaired and painted the *Lesley,* a second-hand boat; this and the *Margaret,* built for the Peates by Mr. Nurser of Braunston, were named after their children. He also altered the *Cressy,* fitting it with a steam engine, and later with a Ford car engine. Eventually the *Cressy* was acquired by Mr. L.T.C. Rolt who travelled in her along most of the canals of England. An account of his journeyings, in which he was accompanied by his wife, are described in his delightful book *Narrow Boat.*

When Mr. Peate was asked if he would use the canal again if it were to be re-opened and properly maintained, he said that this was not likely to happen owing to the lowering of certain road bridges where the water of the canal was piped through underneath; the piping of water for over a mile at Pant owing to leakage; and the unrepaired break in the bank on the Llanymynech branch which occurred in 1936. But the basic reason was one of 'manpower'. Too many men had to be employed on too many boats. If the canal had been made much wider and deeper so that at least 50 ton loads could have been carried, then the position would have been different.

Today the Peates employ bulk grain carriers which can carry a load of 13 tons of grain, and these make two journeys to Liverpool and back most days by road. Only two men are required and the carriers can be loaded up in a quarter of an hour, and unloaded in about the same time. On the average they bring 130 tons of grain each week to the mill. To bring the same quantity of grain by canal used to require seven boats with their seven families; the grain had to be filled into sacks at Ellesmere Port after it had crossed from Liverpool; and it had to be emptied again at the mill. Further, the men were paid according to tonnage; there were the canal's tolls to pay; and there was the cost of the boats' maintenance.

The lack of good roads led to the use of the canal in the early days, and without its aid the mill would have remained isolated and soon shut down. It is rather ironic that the modern development of road transport had caused the closure of the canal and led to an increase in the prosperity of the mill.

The three large Flour Mills erected at Ellesmere Port, have already been discussed in Chapter 4.

Smaller, privately owned mills arose at various places along the canal; but the Maesbury Hall Mill was the only one to develop into a large concern, the others became much smaller provender mills, grinding up maize and other corn to provide animal feeding stuffs. One of these, Sumner's Mill at Wrenbury, is still working; but the others have closed down, and reliable information is difficult to obtain.

The mill at Queen's Head was said to have closed down about 1940. At one time it was a flour mill, using locally grown corn as well as corn brought from Liverpool by canal. About 1912 it supplied Phillip's, grocers of Oswestry, with self-raising flour, and at one time the miller was an agent for Bibbys.

Another mill at Grindley Brook closed down a few years ago.

CHAPTER 10

INDUSTRIES SERVED BY THE ELLESMERE CANAL
5. BRICK AND TILE MAKING; SAND; SUPERPHOSPHATE; & A NOTE ON PASSENGERS

Often where shafts were sunk to obtain coal or iron ore they passed through beds of clay, and if the clay was suitable a brick-making industry often arose. This happened in the Morda Coalfield just south of Oswestry, where there was even a small pottery works. It seems never to have achieved any fame, so its products were probably sold locally. Some of the small coal pits in the Chirk Coalfield possessed brick kilns, and the 1873 Ordnance Survey map shows some at Quinta, although not a sign of them remains today. At Gledrid, almost opposite to the old terminus of the Glyn Valley Tramway, there were brick kilns connected to the canal by a very short tramway - in recent years this site has been converted into a piggery. There was quite a concentration of works connected with the manufacture of bricks and tiles in the neighbourhood of Pontcysyllte. The Pen-y-bont works made bricks, tiles and terra cotta, while the Tref-y-nant works made fireclay bricks, and a third works at Trevor specialised in silica refractory bricks.

The first two works have now closed down, but they still were active in 1955. Being only a short distance away from the canal at the Irish Bridge, where the Cefn Mawr railway viaduct crosses the Dee Valley, the Pen-y-bont works were connected to it by a tramway which is shown on the 1873 Ordnance Survey map. However it was later replaced by a branch railway line connecting with the main Shrewsbury-Chester line just where the viaduct begins, close by the canal.

On leaving the works the old tramway kept close to the road all the way. At the canal its terminus was well above canal level, so possibly the last portion ran down an incline.

At the works the office building was faced with smooth, shiny reddish bricks and tiles, with quite a lot of elaboration and insets of decorated tiles. Unfortunately no documentary information was available. A very steep slope led down into the quarries - these were immense and must have been worked for more than a hundred years. At different levels were buildings where the clay was crushed and graded, and near these a row of large mounds of different grades of clay. Men could be seen at work, and tramways ramified through the quarry. At a tug on a signal wire, a truck loaded with clay began its ascent, being pulled by means of a powerful steam engine to the top of the slope and into the works.

An elderly employee could remember the old tramway in use, although he was vague about the date; and he also remembered narrow boats on the canal being used as tankers to bring the crude tar oil to Monsanto Chemicals, Ltd., where it was used as a source for obtaining carbolic acid. On the way back to the Irish Bridge we walked along the branch railway, and had a magnificent view of the Cefn Viaduct with the Dee flowing under its central arch.

Sand

Along the Llanymynech branch of the canal, to the right and on the far side of the canal bridge between Rednal and Queen's Head, there used to be a sandpit; most of it has been filled in. Not much farther along there was a larger sandpit on the left. The sand from this pit was conveyed to the canal by a little tramway which passed under the Rednal-Queen's Head road, and through a warehouse by the canal. Owing to the small size of the tunnel, which still exists, a donkey was employed to pull the trucks. This sand was of good quality for building purposes and was taken quite long distances along the canal; but this traffic finished many years ago, probably owing to the silting up of the canal which made it impossible for the boats to carry a payload.

Calcium superphosphate fertilizer

One rather unexpected industry near Rednal was the manufacture of superphosphate fertilizer. Details of this industry are difficult to come by, but an advertisement in the *Oswestry Advertizer* for 26 February 1862 states 'Bone Manure Manufactory, Meifod - agent for the Oswestry district, Mr. Richards'. Another advertisement for 7 May 1862 gives agents for this firm at Meifod, Oswestry and Ellesmere. The present manager says that the original works were established in 1858, and that at some time in the 1880s a warehouse by the canal and railway at Rednal was taken over by the Richards and converted to a fertilizer factory, chiefly for making superphosphate. A letter from the son of the former owner mentions that an arm of the canal used to lead to a square-shaped dock close by the railway embankment. However, at the time the factory was established here the canal was cut off by the towpath being made continuous across it, so that boats carrying bones or other source of phosphates and concentrated sulphuric acid came alongside the canal bank, where their cargoes were unloaded into little trucks by means of a hand crane. These trucks were then pushed by hand into the works. Sometime between 1900 and 1910 the Canal Company agreed to open up the arm by installing a swing bridge to take the towpath. This made it possible for boats to come alongside the works and be mechanically unloaded. The works have only recently closed down.

In the heyday of the canals tramways and railways were used to bring commodities to the canal to be loaded into the canal boats; when the railways began to replace canals, it was usually the other way round. However, at the fertilizer works arrangements were made in 1850 to move goods *from* the railway into the canal boats. This was because the Welsh Railways had not been constructed to Llanymynech, Welshpool and Newtown, the area served by the Ellesmere Canal. At this time the canal was leased to the L.N.W.R. and although the railway at Rednal was owned by the G.W.R. it had no means of getting its goods to these Welsh districts except by the canal.

An agreement was made between the canal and railway companies, each company to pay half the cost of the transhipping installations, and fixing the limits of the areas

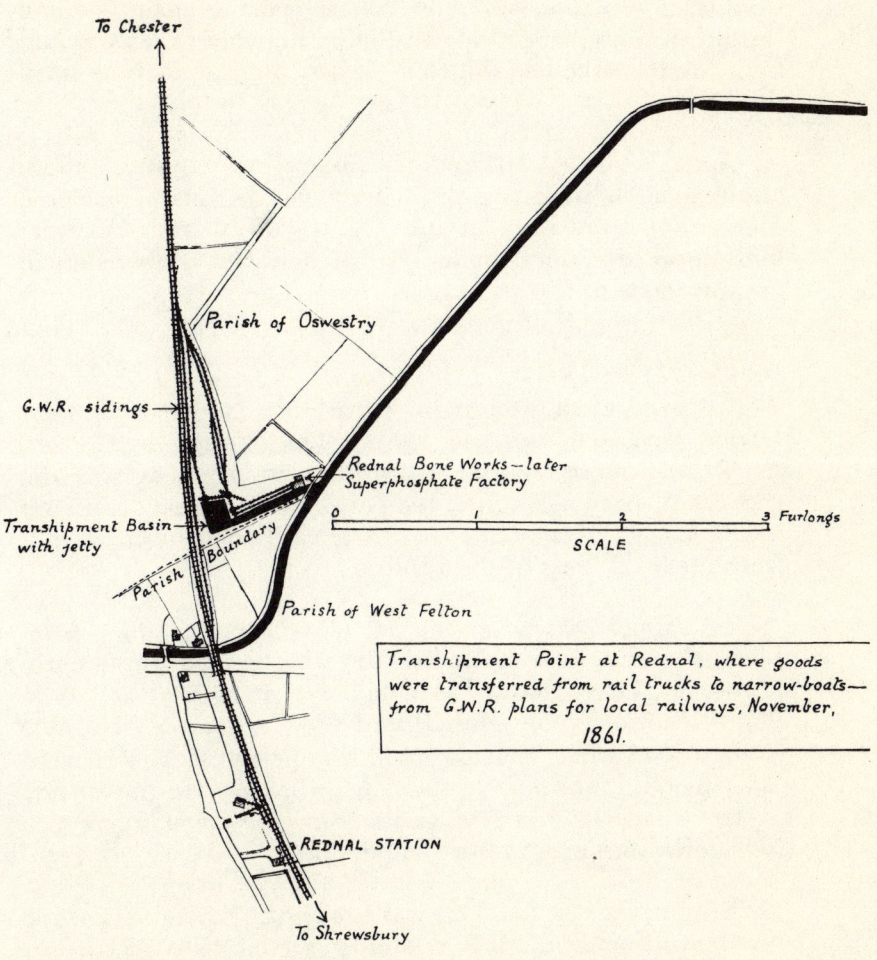

To Chester

Parish of Oswestry

G.W.R. sidings →

Rednal Bone Works — later
Superphosphate Factory

Transhipment Basin →
with jetty

Parish Boundary

Parish of West Felton

0   1   2   3   Furlongs
SCALE

Transhipment Point at Rednal, where goods
were transferred from rail trucks to narrow-boats—
from G.W.R. plans for local railways, November,
1861.

→ REDNAL STATION

To Shrewsbury

to be served. The Canal Company was responsible for digging the basin adjacent to the railway embankment and connecting it by a short arm to the line of the canal, while the Railway Company was to arrange for lines to leave its main line and run down a prepared slope to the basin, where a jetty would be made to make transhipment easier; there was also a small turntable.

There is little information about events after 1850, although a map of a proposed railway in this area, dated 1861, shows the installations. As the Welsh railways were built soon after its completion it is doubtful whether much use was made of the arrangement.

A note on Passengers

As we have already seen, in Chapter 4, a passenger boat service operated on the Wirral Line from the outset. At Rednal an even more surprising arrangement was the transfer of passengers from the railway to the canal, and I am indebted to J. Horsley Denton who unearthed this information from the local Press of the 1850s.

The service was intended for passengers travelling from Liverpool and Birkenhead by the Chester and Shrewsbury Railway. They would leave the train at Rednal and West Felton Station (now closed) and walk a quarter of a mile along a road which met the road leading to Queen's Head at right angles, quite near to the railway bridge. On the far side of this road, only a few yards from the canal, there is a two-storied brick and timbered building.

Denton suggests that this was too lightly built to serve as a warehouse, and in all probability served as a 'Passenger Terminal' for a rapid fly-boat service on the canal plying between Rednal and Newtown. The service did exist - there are timetables to prove it - but the purpose of this building is still in doubt. It was suggested that passengers would enter the top storey which is at road level, get their tickets, go downstairs to the lower storey which is at canal level, and embark.

Plate 17.—'Ice-boat', the 'Ellesmere' aground near Maintenance Depot.
See text for description

Plate 18.—Scene at Ellesmere Maintenance Depot. Note boat dock, with
Beech House beyond, and supports down which the travelling crane used
to run

Plate 19.—At work in lockgate shop, Ellesmere Maintenance Depot

Plate 20.—Inside Boat Dock at Ellesmere. Note large iron weights used in 'indexing' (E.C.Co.=Ellesmere Canal Company; M.C.Co.=Montgomeryshire Canal Company); the two cranes used for lowering the weights into the boats; and a copper indexing strip

Plate 21.—The travelling crane in the Ellesmere Depot Yard, lowering a lockgate on to a narrow boat for transport to the Wharf. 24 Sept. 1956

Plate 22.—Mr. Jack Roberts with 'Molly' drawing the narrow boat 'Antwerp' under the Red Bridge at Ellesmere. It was used as a general purpose work boat. 25 Aug. 1952

Plate 23.—Entrance to the Ellesmere Canal Tunnel. Note stop-plank
shelter on left. 17 Apr. 1952

Plate 24.—The double lock at Welsh Frankton
—now disused

Plate 25.—The last resting place of the packet boat 'Duchess-Countess' at Welsh Frankton before being broken up. 16 Sept. 1952

Plate 26.—Sweeney colliery tramway showing sleeper blocks still in original position where it passed under old Cambrian railway line from Oswestry to Welshpool. 4 Apr. 1956

Plate 27.—Peat stacks on Fenns Moss. The canal passes through part of this Moss. 2 May 1949

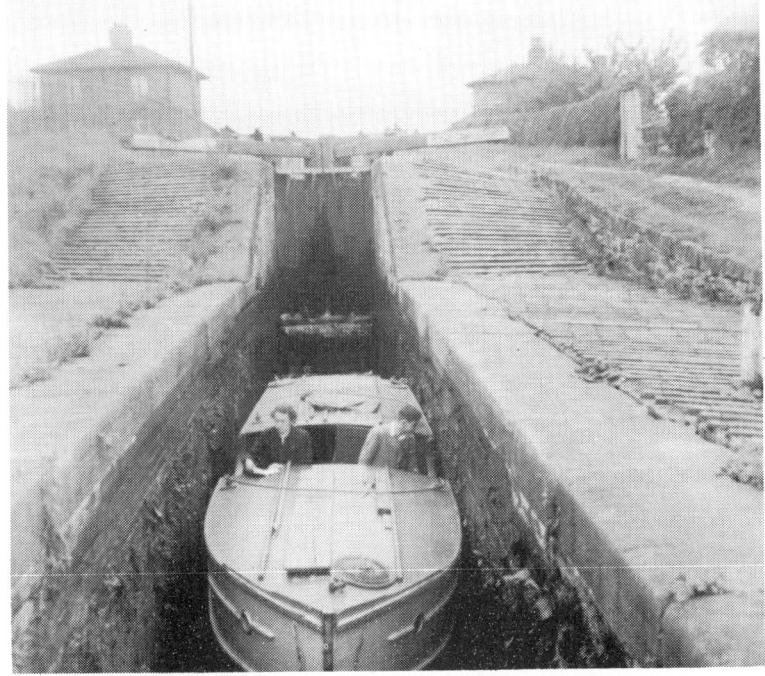

Plate 28.—Negotiating the Grindley Brook lock-staircase in the 'Beryl' on our voyage. 1952

Plate 29.—Pen-y-graig limestone quarries, Vroncysyllte. Two trucks loaded with quarried limestone about to start the long descent from the quarry face. 9 Apr. 1954

Plate 30.—'Living History'. Horse-drawn transport of quarried limestone at Pen-y-graig quarry. Note two trucks open on one side, are used

Plate 31.—Derelict haulage drum, Pant, at the head of an incline leading down to the canal. Note limestone wall supports and original chain still present. 19 Apr. 1955

Plate 32.—Block of three limekilns at Hampton Bank. 1 May 1951

In spite of its rather delicate appearance from the outside, the building is extremely solid inside, having very strong joists and floor boards, and - there is *no connection between the two stories*. There is a covered stairway on the outside of the building in the last stages of disrepair. It is clear that it led down to the side entrance of the lower storey. There is no indication of any previous fittings for the passengers or stalls and mangers for the horses.

It seems unlikely that such a substantial two storied building would be needed for passengers - a mere shed, rather like a bus shelter would have sufficed. Now empty, there is evidence that it did serve as a warehouse in the past, and it could have had the double purpose of warehouse and passenger terminal.

The timetables show that after leaving Rednal the boat stopped at Queen's Head, Maesbury, Pant Bridge, Llanymynech, Carreghofa, New Bridge, Four Crosses, Burgedin, Brithdir, Berriew, Garthmill, Brynderwyn, Foundry Bridge, finally finishing its journey at Newtown.

The extraordinary feature of this canal service was its speed, because the itinerary included 22 locks in a distance of 32 miles. With the stops given above it completed this journey in 5 hours 12 min. Speed was attained by using at least two horses, with fresh horses held in readiness at stables along the line. The boatman would sound a horn to warn the lock-keeper of his approach so that the locks could be prepared for the immediate entrance of the boat; and there would be a right of way at all bridges. Even so, Horsley Denton is of the opinion that to maintain the given schedule, speeds of 10 - 15 miles per hour must have been reached between some of the locks! Of course there was no engine to reverse so that the boat would have to begin to slow down at quite a distance from the next lock.

Engined boats at speed cause a wash which is very destructive to the banks, but this effect is not nearly so marked in the case of horse-drawn boats travelling fast. A further point suggested is that in a well designed fly-boat the bow might tend to rise out of the water so that the boat was virtually aquaplaning.

CHAPTER 11

CANAL CONSTRUCTION AND MAINTENANCE

Canals were dug with sloping sides and flat bottoms, and then lined with 'puddled clay', i.e. clay which has been mixed with water until it attains the consistency of a 'mud pie', and is sufficiently stiff to retain its shape - this is well shown in the photograph of repairs near Wenffryd Bridge. Puddled clay forms a waterproof layer. The clay for the Ellesmere Canal came from the clay pits along the Press branch. Leakages sometimes occurred, due to subsidence in areas where coal or salt were mined, or to the growth of tree roots, or to removing too much material when dredging. Quite a lot of soil and stones was washed down the sides of cuttings in the early days before the growth of vegetation consolidated the slopes; feeder streams brought in sediment; and periodic removal of spilled coal at coal wharves or road stone at other wharves was found to be necessary.

Sometimes leakages increased until a catastrophic break in the bank occurred. It was the lengthman's duty to keep a watch on the state of the banks so that repairs could be carried out before it was too late, but if a break occurred he quickly made dams of 'stop-planks' on either side of the break as described in Chapter 5. These dams were quite effective, but were not absolutely watertight, so a small pumping engine was employed to pump out the water which leaked through the dams.

On occasions, a really big break might occur in a high embankment - one occurred near Millar's Bridge on the 'Water Line' near Llangollen on 7 September 1960 and carried down fully grown trees with it; while an earlier break between Sun Trevor and Wenffryd Bridge, also on the 'Water Line', washed away a portion of the railway line which ran along immediately below the canal - the repair of this break is also shown in the photograph mentioned above. By the time the Millar's Bridge break occurred it was possible to employ contractors using bull-dozers and earth-transporting machines and so finish the job much more quickly than before. One area where many breaks have occurred in the past is Whixall Moss, where the unstable, slippery peat causes trouble; while at Beeston, on the old Chester Canal, Telford had to build a new lock entirely of iron in 1828, because the old one was built on a quicksand foundation and the periodic rising of the ground water nearly destroyed the old lock foundations.

A great many bridges had to be built. There were 'road bridges' to take roads over the canal, and 'accommodation bridges' needed to connect the parts of a farmer's land severed by the canal. A standard type of bridge was evolved - it was usually humped-back, a nuisance to us today but not so in the more leisurely days of horse traffic. When Shade Oak bridge on the Welsh Frankton - Weston Lullingfields section of the canal was being demolished on 23 April 1951 it was possible to see that the brick arch consisted of a single layer of bricks, placed with their long axes at right angles to the arch, and then covered over with rubble; a stone capped brick parapet was added at the sides. Today, many of these bridges have been demolished, and others replaced by flatter, iron and concrete bridges, more suited to modern traffic. Where the flattening has been severe the canal water has been piped under the road, as at Queen's Head on the Llanymynech section of the Ellesmere Canal.

The brick arch continued vertically down under the water to meet a flat, horizontal base; while outside the bridge the 'wing walls' were parallel at first where the iron-shod grooves for receiving the stop-planks were situated, and then swung outwards until the canal became wide enough for two narrow boats to pass. The earthen banks have been made more secure in recent years by driving in iron or concrete piling. There is a movable type of bridge which occurs on the Ellesmere Canal called a 'lift-up bridge'. It is made of wood, and the part on which one crosses the canal is hinged at bank level, while from the opposite side two chains ascend to a horizontal superstructure, pivoted at its midpoint to the top of a rigid, upright framework. To balance the bridge there is a compartment filled with pieces of iron, etc., at the far end of the pivoted superstructure, and a chain hanging down from it. The whole affair is so well balanced that a pull on the chain will raise the bridge quite easily.

Locks were expensive and had to be made long enough and wide enough to take a 70 ft. narrow boat of nearly 7 ft. beam; the depth depended on the lie of the land, but was often about 10 ft.. If the level altered steeply it was necessary to build a 'lock staircase' where the locks were built as a multiple unit; for instance there is a staircase of three locks at Grindley Brook, in which the intermediate gates are common to the adjacent locks. Just below this staircase there are three separate locks and these are separated by short lengths of canal known as 'pounds'. Other staircase units are the 'double locks' at Bunbury on the old Chester Canal section, and at Welsh Frankton on the Ellesmere Canal.

The holiday maker on the canal soon becomes familiar with the working of lock 'paddles'. These are simply openings covered by a wood paddle sliding in iron grooves; water pressure makes these quite hard to move, and so the iron rod attached to them finishes at the upper end in a ratchet, which can be raised by means of a handle engaging with a pinion wheel. The paddles are of two kinds; (a) 'gate paddles' in the lockgate, the paddle opening being partially covered by iron plating so as to deflect the inflow of water away from the boat, and (b) 'ground paddles' where a small culvert leads water to the paddle to enter the lock below water level - this puts no strain on the lockgates.

In Chapter 5 an account of the manufacture of wooden lockgates was given; and in Chapter 3 Telford's use of iron in the erection of the Longdon-on-Tern Aqueduct, the Chirk and Pontcysyllte Aqueducts, and the Buildwas Bridge was described. Always on the watch for new outlets for iron, Telford used it for making further bridges, such as the Waterloo Bridge at Betws-y-Coed and the beautiful Craig-ellachie Bridge over the River Tay in Scotland. He also advocated the use of iron for lockgates. In an examination of the canal in 1821 by a special Committee we read,

> The four locks at Frankton have all upper gates of cast iron, and one pair of lower gates of the same material. These iron gates were the first constructed, and they have answered well, but they have been improved upon in those subsequently made.
> The three locks at Aston Moor are in an excellent state of repair. The gates are all of cast iron. The two locks at New Marton Moor are also in a good state, especially the upper ones, which has its gates entirely of cast iron. The upper gate of the lower lock is also of cast iron.

The same report also says,

> The iron gates to the Tide Lock at Ellesmere Port, and those at Aston and New Marton Locks, have been fitted and hung, with an accuracy not surpassed, if equalled, by any of the wooden ones.

and,

> The cast iron gates have been supplied by Mr. Hazeldine, the vicinity of whose foundry to the canal enables him to supply them cheaper, and more conveniently, than any other person, and they appear to your Committee to be cast with much accuracy.

In his *Autobiography* Telford gives costs and states, 'some of these gates have been in use upwards of 20 years, and show no symptoms of decay.'

For some reason which is not clear, iron gates were given up and wooden gates appeared once more. In September 1959 there were no iron lockgates on the Ellesmere and Chester Canal, and the upper gates at Welshpool lock on the Montgomeryshire Canal were the sole surviving iron lockgates of the Telford age in this part of the country; even these have now been removed. However, in recent years steel has appeared in place of wood and cast-iron. At Grindley Brook the last wooden lockgate was made at Ellesmere in 1956, and in the lock staircase only the bottom gates are now made of wood, whilst the others are made of steel, two having been installed in 1962, one in 1963, one in 1966, and one in 1970. The New Marton topgate was replaced in steel in 1968, and the topgates at Willey Moor, Marbury and Baddiley in 1963, 1970 and 1966. It may be that expense is the reason for these replacements, for 5 tons of English oak is an expensive item today.

Telford's use of iron even included the introduction of

iron narrow boats, and a few of these still persist as main-tenance boats, although they now have wooden bottoms.

The flow of water in canals is very slow and canals sometimes get frozen over. This was serious when canals were the main arteries of transport, and special 'ice-boats' (i.e. 'ice-breakers') were built. For several years the ice-boat 'Ellesmere' was aground in the canal near to the Ellesmere Depot. It had a slatted wooden deck with a strong post at each end, supporting a stout, horizontally placed bar; the bow was protected by iron. Ice-boats were stationed at various points along the canal and had regular beats.

The *Whitchurch* was stationed above the locks at Grindley Brook, and worked from there to Whixall Moss, including the Whitchurch Arm. The *Whitemere,* stationed at Whixall Moss, worked along as far as Bettisfield, including the Prees Branch. The *Ellesmere,* stationed at Ellesmere, worked from Bettis-field, through Ellesmere to Frankton, including the Weston Line. The *Glyn* worked from Pontcysyllte to Welsh Frankton.

When an 'ice-boat' was brought into the Ellesmere Boat Dock for repair its construction could readily be seen. First of all, unlike narrow boats which have flat bottoms, the ice-boats have a normal boat-shaped hull. When stripped for repair the tarred wooden hull could be seen, covered with felt, and finally with vertical strips of tinplate overlapping in a backward direction. The hull was then tarred over.

In use several men stood on the deck on either side of the iron bar, and, gripping this firmly, rocked the boat from side to side to break up the ice, while six horses strained their hardest to keep the boat going forward. The man at the tiller endeavoured to steer a direct course.

L.T.C. Rolt, in his book *Narrow Boat,* paints the scene vividly,

Two gangs of breakers made a spectacular arrival at Banbury.....
Long before they came in sight their approach was heralded by a grinding and crashing sound, then round the bend came the sweating horses keeping a fine pace as though entering into the spirit of the adventure.

Finally, the boat itself appeared, rolling almost gunwale under from the efforts of her heaving crew, who, ruddy faced from the cold wind and strenuous labour, seemed oblivious alike to the jets of icy water which spurted from overside and the dirty puddle which slopped to and fro beneath their feet. At the tiller stood an elderly lengthsman, balancing first on one leg, then on the other as he endeavoured to keep the bucketing craft upon some semblance of a course.

These boats are no longer used today and are items for the industrial archaeologist.

With a few exceptions the canals in England are of two types, narrow boat canals and barge canals. Because canals were costly to make they were kept as narrow as possible, and the numerous bridges were only just able to pass one narrow boat with its beam of nearly 7 ft. - this width also applied to tunnels and aqueducts. In order to increase the cargo carrying capacity the lengths of narrow boats were increased until they were almost 70 ft. long, at which length they could carry approximately 25 - 30 tons of cargo. The length could not be increased further because of the difficulty of negotiating bends in the canal, and the longer locks would have been too costly. For turning round, special bays had to be made in the bank termed 'winding holes'. Usually narrow boats worked in pairs, the second boat ('butty') being towed passively behind the leading boat.

All the above features on a barge canal, such as the Wirral Line, were double the width of those on a narrow canal. Two narrow boats were able to pass through their locks side by side, an advantage which, unfortunately, would not work in reverse as the 14 ft. beam of a barge prevented it from entering the locks on the narrow canals. Only a few of our canals are used commercially today, because only a few of them are wide enough to carry worthwhile cargoes.

CHAPTER 12

MID-CHESHIRE USES THE CANAL
AS AN OPEN PIPE-LINE

Unlike rivers, canals can climb over watersheds, but this does not mean that water can flow uphill! Nor for that matter does the water in a length of canal flow downhill. A canal simply consists of a series of level stretches separated by locks, and these are the devices in which the water level is altered.

Take a boat travelling in an upward direction. When it reaches a lock it finds it either empty or full of water. If the lock is full, 'paddles' in the lower lockgates are opened to let the water out until the level of the canal below the lock and inside the lock are the same. The result is that a lockful of water has been transferred from a higher level to a lower level. The bottom lockgates can now be opened and the boat brought into the lock. After closing the bottom paddles the upper paddles can be opened to fill up the lock once more, raising the boat to the level of the canal above the lock. If the lock is empty on arrival the boat can enter as soon as the gates are opened, and the lock will then be filled with water as before. It means that in either case a lockful of water has been lost from the higher level.

If you work out the procedure when the boat, having surmounted the watershed, descends to a lower level, you will find the result is the same, namely, that the passage of a boat through a lock results in water being lost from the higher levels. The highest level of all, termed the 'summit level', is therefore constantly losing water in both directions and this has to be replaced, otherwise it would soon be dried out.

The early canal builders always tried to make a long summit level, and tried to replenish it by means of lakes, streams, or even by pumping up water from coalmines. Where none of these were present, they built reservoirs. One of the objections to the Western Canal Scheme for the Ellesmere Canal was the great number of locks needed, and the absence of any large sized lakes to act as reservoirs, although one is mentioned in the hills two miles above the Poolmouth Valley as,

> a great reservoir which will contain nearly 200 acres; an embankment may be made with 30 ft. depth of water at one end, and 16 at the other; it would be advisable to throw an embankment at the Poolmouth Valley . . . as a secondary reservoir.

The Frood Branch was part of a branch line on this canal intended to reach this reservoir; but as we have read in Chapter 2 the three mile branch did not last long, and the reservoir was never constructed.

The Wirral Line of the canal was on a level with no locks except at each end, where it descended to the Mersey and the Dee. Negotiations with the Chester Canal authorities resulted in a certain amount of water being obtained from the Chester Canal, but this was not enough; and as already mentioned, a Boulton and Watt steam engine, manufactured under licence by John Wilkinson, was installed at Ellesmere Port to pump back the water lost by the passage of boats. A note states 'The Wirral Fire Engine throws up 2,596 gallons per minute'.

While the canal was being dug from Vroncysyllte on the south bank of the River Dee southwards to Welsh Frankton, and from there to Weston Lullingfields in one direction and to Llanymynech in another, there was really no adequate supply of water, and every small source was utilized. In a *Report* by Jessop dated 14 July 1795 we read,

> As there is reason to expect a considerable trade on the canal before water can be brought from the reservoir over the great Aqueduct, it will be necessary to take in part of the Morlas River.

In fact the Morlas 'river' was quite a small brook. Another only slightly larger brook which was also used was the Morda Brook; one or two tiny streams were brought into operation as well, such as one opposite to the Black Park Colliery inlet. However this caused difficulties because, small though these streams were, they were used as sources

of power for working many mills along their courses. There
was no trouble during the winter or in stormy weather, when
their flow became torrential and often resulted in flooding,
but the supply of water during the summer was fitful and
inadequate.

It is interesting to find in this *Report* of Jessop an idea
which was later carried out and became the canal's sole
source of water. It reads as follows,

> Until now I had not been informed that near the source of the Dee
> there is an extensive lake called Bala Pool; this has suggested an idea,
> that at a small expense water, in lieu of the Morlas, may be given to
> the Dee using this Pool as a reservoir, either by making provision for
> drawing off 6 inches in the depth of this Pool, or by raising it 6
> inches, or by both, and this, I apprehend, may be done without
> any possible injury to any property.

While the Western Canal Scheme was still being entertained,
this alternative source of water was not seriously considered;
in fact, the Act needed for tapping this supply of water was
not obtained until 24 June 1804, and a tremendous effort
was then made to get this 'Water Line' constructed in time
for the official opening of the Pontcysyllte Aqueduct in
1805. However, it proved to be a difficult task, and water
from the River Dee did not flow over the Aqueduct until the
completion of the 'Water Line' in 1808.

As the Aqueduct was opened on time the question of
where its water came from remains to be answered. There
seems to be no information available to answer it. An
examination of a map of this area shows plenty of coalmines
nearby, but no means of bringing water pumped out of them
to the north end of the Aqueduct. There is a sizeable brook
called the Tref-y-nant Brook which rises in the Ruabon
mountains north of the Trevor Rocks and passes quite close
to the Aqueduct, and there seems little doubt that this must
have been used until the 'Water Line' had been completed.

Water for the canal was obtained at Llantisilio by building
a weir (popularly known as the *Horseshoe Falls* from its
shape) across the river Dee. The weir extended from the
south bank of the river, but did not reach the north bank
until it had side tracked water through the Meter House at
the start of the canal. At first there was no limit on the

amount of water extracted from the Dee as long as an equivalent quantity was let into the Dee at the Bala Sluices - these were under the Company's control - but in 1944 the amount allowable was fixed at 6¼ million gallons a day by Act of Parliament.

The primary purpose of the canal was for navigation, and in the early days it was illegal to use water for any other purpose. However farmers and later on railway concerns used it, and some industrial concerns.

The 1944 Act was a very comprehensive measure which looked like ringing the death knell for the local canals: it gave permission for the closing of the whole of the Mont-gomeryshire Canal and its Guilsfield branch; on the Ellesmere Canal the Llanymynech branch and the Weston branch, besides the line from Hurleston Junction going through Whitchurch, Ellesmere and Chirk to Llantisilio, along with the Prees branch; and on the Shrewsbury Canal the line from Shrewsbury to Donnington, the Newport Canal, and the remaining section of the Shropshire Canal.

Only one canal in the above list was spared, and that was the part of the Ellesmere Canal running from Hurleston Junction through Whitchurch, Ellesmere, Chirk and Llangollen to Llantisilio, since rechristened *'The Llangollen Canal'*. It was an eleventh hour decision which saved this part of the canal for the use and enjoyment of future generations, as the Act for its abandonment was obtained in 1944, and for its reprieve in 1954. Why was it spared?

It was spared because of the need of large towns for water. The increased demands for water by Water Boards had not been forseen, but in 1950 several Water Boards collaborated to get a Bill passed enabling them to extract more water from the Dee. To carry out these objects the sluices at the outlet of Lake Bala were moved to a different position to enable the waters of another stream to be brought back into the lake; secondly, the outlet level of the sluices was lowered. In refreshingly simple language Counsel explained the effect of this as follows.

It is like this, if you have a barrel, and you have a bung halfway up the barrel, you can only empty the top half of the barrel. If you lower the bung to threequarters of the way down the barrel, you can draw out threequarters of the capacity of the barrel. Thus, by lowering the level of the outlet you are able to draw off, for the purpose of replenishment of the river in the summer dry periods, this bottom layer of water in the reservoir.

An extra 40 million gallons per day was obtained in this way.

Monsanto's Chemical Works at Cefn Mawr had relied on canal water, and when there was a break in the canal bank near Llangollen they found themselves in such a serious position that they had to insist on water being pumped past the break to reach them. After this incident they built their own pumping station by the Dee just beyond Pontcysyllte - it can readily be seen fromtthe Aqueduct - so that they became independent of the canal for their water supply.

Of far greater importance for the future of the canal was the fact that the Mid and Southeast Cheshire Water Board was authorized to convey water from the River Dee at Vroncysyllte to the canal reservoir at Hurleston Junction for abstraction there. On reaching Hurleston Reservoir it is thoroughly purified before being distributed to Mid and Southeast Cheshire. The Water Board reckon that they will have saved three quarters of a million pounds by using the canal as an 'open pipeline', and so not having to provide steel piping to do the carrying.

How Mid and Southeast Cheshire get a supply of 'potable water' (i.e. water fit to drink) from raw river water is as follows. The canal authorities were responsible for the conveyance of river water from the Dee, while the Water Board was responsible for the erection of the pumping station at Vroncysyllte and of the purification plant at Hurleston Reservoir. The reason for having the pumping station at Vroncysyllte to the east of the Aqueduct, is that considerable trouble was experienced in the past with leakage of water along the 'Water Line' of the canal; also the Aqueduct was of too small dimensions to take more than double the amount of water which the new scheme envisaged.

The pump house is quite close to the Aqueduct, but is somewhat hidden by trees. After the water has passed through screens and a Venturi Meter it is pumped along a concrete rising main to the canal near to the lift-up bridge at Vroncysyllte on the south side of the Dee Valley.

The amount of water pumped into the canal by this means is eight million gallons a day.

On reaching the reservoir at Hurleston the water flows into it down an intake which was rebuilt in a stepped formation to encourage aeration of the water. Standing in the reservoir itself is the *Raw Water Pump House* from which the water is pumped to the treatment works. These consist of (a) twelve hopper-shaped *Sedimentation Tanks,* where the water rises from the bottom and meets a dose of alum and activated silica; this has a coagulating effect on the particles carried by the water. The clear water at the top then passes on to (b) *Rapid Gravity Filters.* There are four of these open concrete tanks which have three feet of graded sand in the bottom. This filters the water before it collects in the sump of the main pump house. Lime is added to correct any acidity, and a heavy dose of chlorine to ensure destruction of all bacteria. The water is then pumped to (c) the *Clear Water Contact Reservoir* which has a capacity of two million gallons; as it leaves this it is dechlorinated with sulphur dioxide, but a residual amount of chlorine is left in as a safety measure. The water then flows to (d) the *Main Pump* for distribution. The sludge from the sedimentation tanks and rapid gravity filters is taken to sludge tanks by the lower canal, and finally the supernatant water is returned to the canal, and the concentrated sludge is pumped to sludge drying beds.

The water is now pure enough to drink and is distributed to the Gorsty Hill, Smallwood and Ridley Reservoirs for supplying the needs of Nantwich, Crewe, Middlewich and Sandbach.

We have now reached the interesting position that this canal, built solely for navigational purposes about 165 years ago, remains partly open, and is likely to continue so, as a source of water supply to agriculturalists, industrialists, railway companies and even water supply companies.

CHAPTER 13

A CRUISE ON THE CANAL IN 1952

My family and I had studied the Ellesmere Canal for several years, but had never travelled on it when, in 1952, there seemed to be a distinct possibility of its closure; so we decided to have a family holiday afloat. At that time there were not many boat-hire firms, but we managed to hire the four-berth motor-cruiser, *Beryl*, from the Inland Cruising Association's (now Inland Hire Cruisers) mooring station at Christleton on the old Chester Canal.

When we arrived at Christleton on 13 September 1952 we were given a short instructional trip and then the boat was handed over to our sole charge. Feeling very self-conscious and not a little apprehensive, we started our voyage in an easterly direction. After a quarter of an hour we ran aground! However, we were soon underway again and before long approaching Salmon's Bridge. Here we saw another motor-cruiser, *Romany*, approaching; so playing for safety, we slowed down and then reversed the engine, intending to bring the boat to a firm halt, but found that the rudder had no effect on the stationary craft, so we drifted and nearly collided with the other boat as it came through the bridge! Soon afterwards, however, at Golden Nook Bridge, we let the narrow boat *Bosphorus* pass through more safely.

As time passed we became more confident and were able to relax and survey our surroundings as we made rather monotonous progress through the flat Cheshire plain, occasionally disturbing a heron from its motionless posture on the towpath. At our approach it would slowly rise, leisurely fly some distance ahead and settle again on the towpath.

At this date a number of commercial craft still regularly plied the Chester Canal between Ellesmere Port and the Midlands, so the water was disturbed and muddy, with few weeds.

This canal was built for barge traffic (see page 107) so its locks are massive, its bridges wide. Some of the old, humped-backed brick bridges had been replaced by others made of iron or reinforced concrete; but some, with such attractive names as Crow's Nest, Bate's Mill and Golden Nook yet remained.

After two hours' travelling we reached our first lock, Wharton's Lock, at 6.30 in the evening. We had worked out locking procedure on paper, but decided to have tea before putting theory into practice. Then, with some trepidation, we set to work. There was not a soul in sight. As the lock was full we first had to empty it by opening the paddles in the bottom gates, one of which would not function properly; furthermore, so much water entered through the leaking top gates that it took a long time before the lock was completely emptied. Slowly we pushed the lower gates open and brought the *Beryl* in. We felt that now the worst was over, and after closing the bottom gates and their paddles, opened the topgate paddles and had the satisfaction of seeing our boat rising to a higher level as the water rushed in. By the end of the trip we had worked through 54 locks but there is nothing like the experience of doing something for the very first time, and the memory of our first locking operation carried out in the deepening dusk remains vivid.

It was necessary to find a suitable mooring site without delay - not so easy in semi-darkness. The canal shallowed so rapidly that we could not get near enough to the bank to land without using the gangplank, and the ground proved to be very broken and extremely muddy. It was quite dark by the time we had finished, but a welcome cup of cocoa made a fitting finale to an eventful day.

The next day was Sunday and as we had all wakened up early we decided to do a few miles before breakfast. It was 7.5 a.m. when we cranked up the engine and cast off. The sun was up and the morning mist over the water was lifting so that we could now see Beeston Crag towering up from the level of the plain, surmounted by the ruins of an old castle. Peckforton Castle also could be seen a short distance further south.

Soon we reached Beeston Iron Lock. The original locks caused a great deal of trouble and expense, and in a *Report* dated 1821 we find,

An expense of about £200 was last year incurred in securing the foundations of the locks at Beeston Brook, which are built upon quicksand. The water, having found its way through the platform, had carried with it great quantities of sand, and so far undermined the walls as nearly to occasion the destruction of the lower lock.

This trouble was so persistent that, at the instigation of Telford, in 1828 the old lock was replaced by one made entirely of cast iron plates fitted together, forming, in effect, an iron box.

By 9 o'clock we reached Bunbury Double Lock and breakfasted here while watching a busload of fishermen get ready for a day's sport. Further on, at Calveley, road, rail and canal ran alongside each other but there were no signs of activity, although at one time this must have been an important transhipment point. Barbridge was definitely an important location as the Middlewich Canal connecting the Chester to the Trent and Mersey Canal left here. The canal narrowed down to half its width as it passed under a massive roof spanning wharves and warehouses on both banks, with the lettering 'Edward Dean, Millers' clearly marked (this spanning structure has now been taken down).

Soon the high banks of Hurleston Reservoir rose up on our right; and then we swung round into the basin and could see the high, narrow lockgates at the entrance to the major portion of the Ellesmere Canal, reminding us that it was built to serve the interest of a rural community with locks passing only one narrow boat at a time.

There were four locks separated by short 'pounds' or basins at this junction, and our boat had to rise up through them. Entering the first lock was like entering a narrow canyon; water dripped down from the weathered brick walls far above us; no sunlight reached us at the bottom of this chasm; and the nearness of the walls caused the beat of our engine to reverberate loudly - a rather eerie sensation!

We had been warned that sometimes the water in the old Ellesmere Canal was very low, and unfortunately this was one of those times. When water had been let out of the

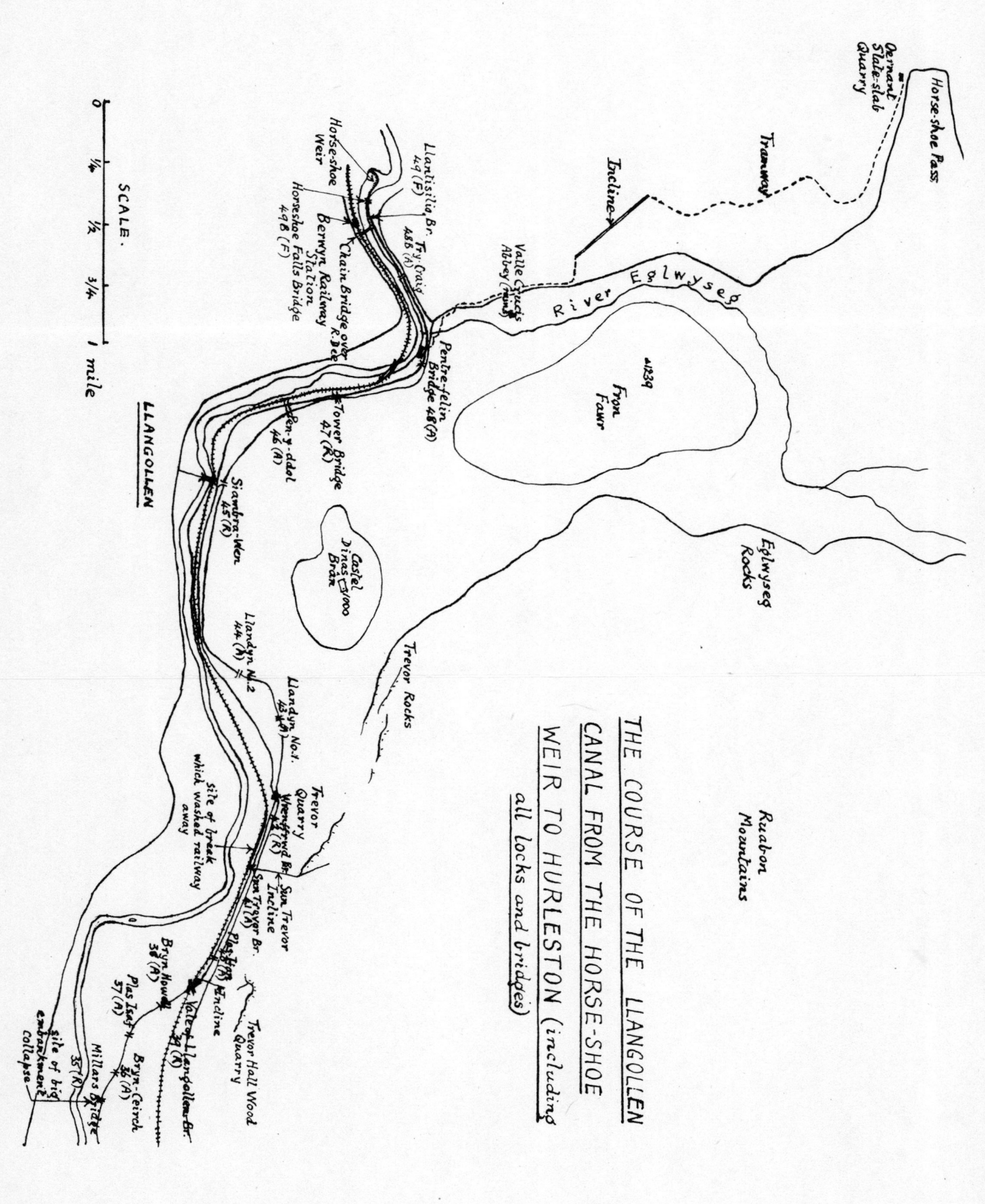

THE COURSE OF THE LLANGOLLEN
CANAL FROM THE HORSE-SHOE
WEIR TO HURLESTON (including
all locks and bridges)

SCALE.

0   ¼   ½   ¾   1 mile

LLANGOLLEN

Horse-shoe Pass

Oernant
Slate-slab
Quarry

Tramway

Incline

Valle Crucis
Abbey (ruins)

River Eglwyseg

Eglwyseg
Rocks

Ruabon
Mountains

1234
Fron Fawr

Trevor Rocks

Castel
Dinas
Bran
1000

Horse-shoe
Weir

Llantisilio Br.
49 (F)

Ty-Craig
48B (A)

Berwyn Railway
Station

Chain Bridge over
R. Dee

Horseshoe Falls Bridge
49B (F)

Pentrefelin
Bridge 48 (A)

Tower Bridge
47 (R)

Pen-y-ddol
46 (A)

Siambra-Wen
45 (R)

Llandyn
44 (R)

Llandyn No.2

Llandyn No.1
43 (A)

Trevor
Quarry

Wrexford Br.
42 (R)

Sun Trevor
Incline

Sun Trevor Br.
41 (R)

Plas yn Pentre
40 (R) Incline

site of breach
which washed railway
away

Bryn Howell
38 (A)

Plas Isaf
37 (A)

Valle Llangollen Br.
39 (R)

Trevor Hall Wood

Trevor Hall
Quarry

Bryn-Ceirch
36 (A)

Millars Bridge
35 (R)

site of big
embankment
collapse

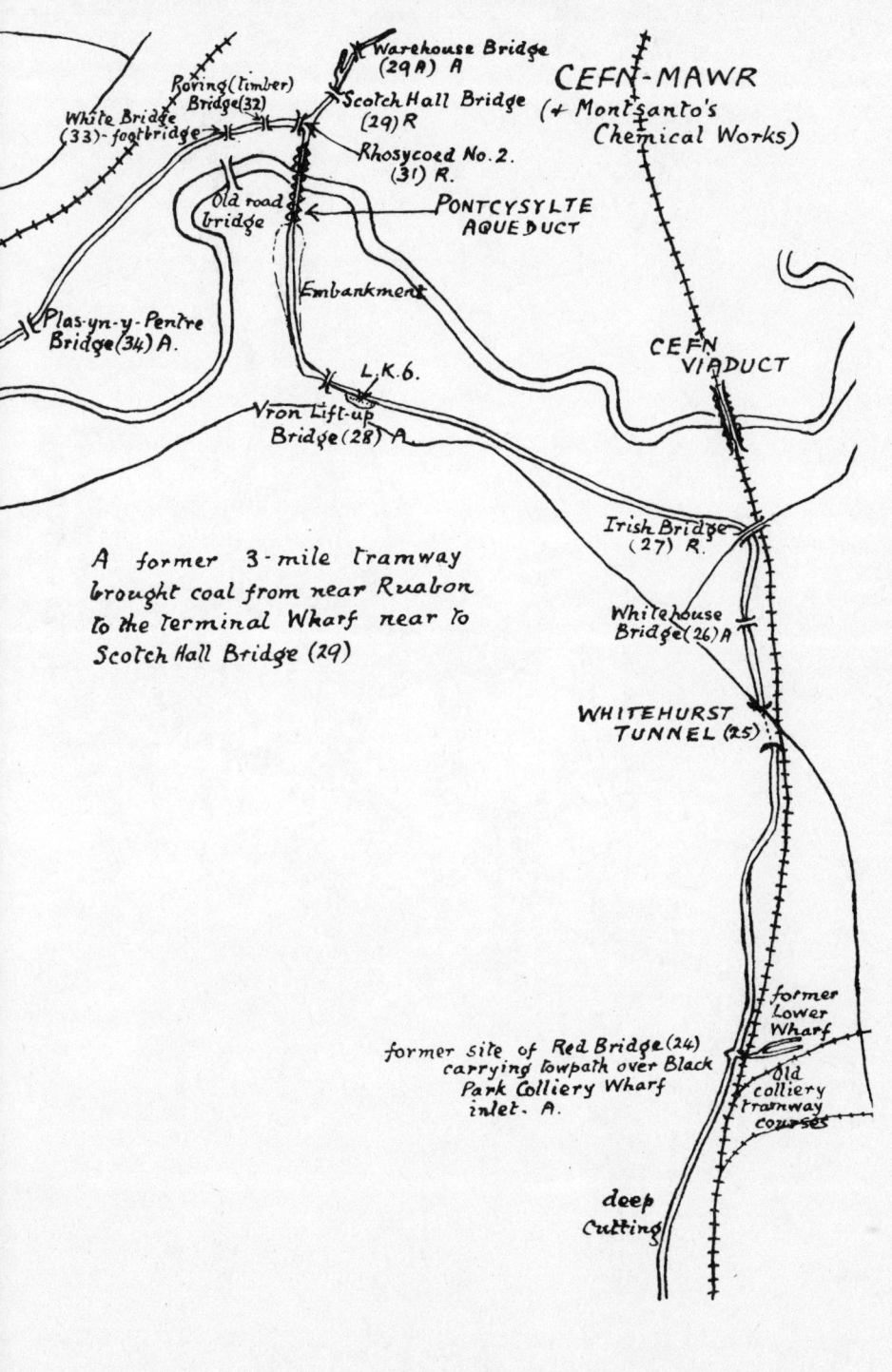

Warehouse Bridge
(29A) A

CEFN-MAWR
(+ Monsanto's
Chemical Works)

Roving (timber)
Bridge (32)

Scotch Hall Bridge
(29) R

White Bridge
(33)-footbridge

Rhosycoed No. 2.
(31) R.

Old road
bridge

PONTCYSYLTE
AQUEDUCT

Embankment

CEFN
VIADUCT

Plas-yn-y-Pentre
Bridge (34) A.

L. K. 6.

Vron Lift-up
Bridge (28) A.

Irish Bridge
(27) R.

A former 3-mile tramway
brought coal from near Ruabon
to the terminal Wharf near to
Scotch Hall Bridge (29)

Whitehouse
Bridge (26) A

WHITEHURST
TUNNEL (25)

former
Lower
Wharf

former site of Red Bridge (24)
carrying towpath over Black
Park Colliery Wharf
inlet. A.

Old
colliery
tramway
courses

deep
Cutting

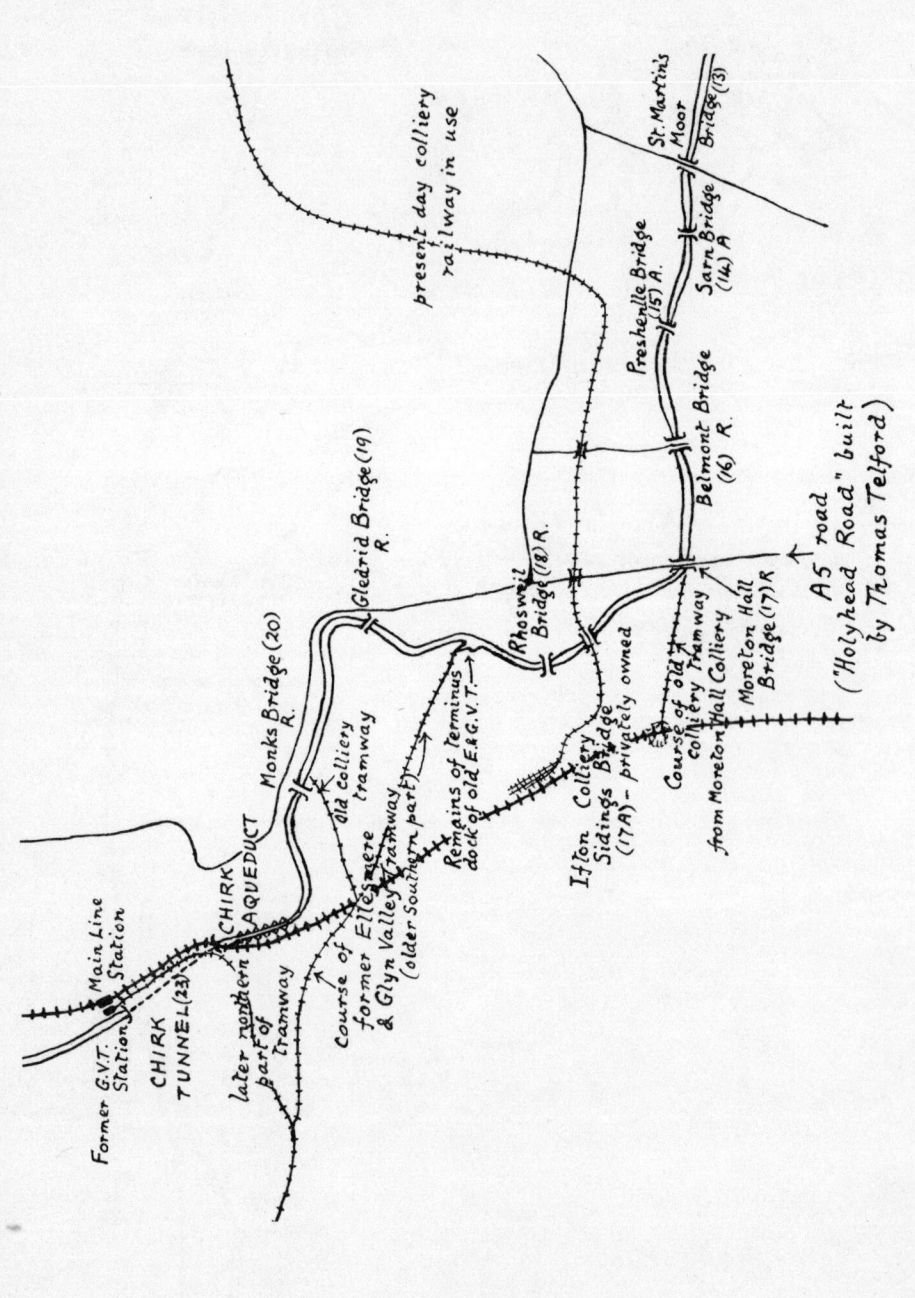

present day colliery railway in use

St. Martin's Moor

Sarn Bridge (13)

Preshenlle Bridge (15) A.

Sarn Bridge (14) A

Belmont Bridge (16) R.

Gledrid Bridge (19) R.

Monks Bridge (20) R.

Rhoswiel Bridge (18) R.

A5 road ("Holyhead Road" built by Thomas Telford)

Moreton Hall Bridge (17) R.

Ifton Colliery Sidings Bridge (17A) - privately owned

Course of old colliery tramway from Moreton Hall Colliery

Old colliery tramway

Remains of Terminus dock of old E.R.G.V.T.

Course of former Ellesmere & Glyn Valley Tramway (older Southern part)

CHIRK AQUEDUCT

later northern part of Tramway

Main Line Station

Former G.V.T. Station

CHIRK TUNNEL (23)

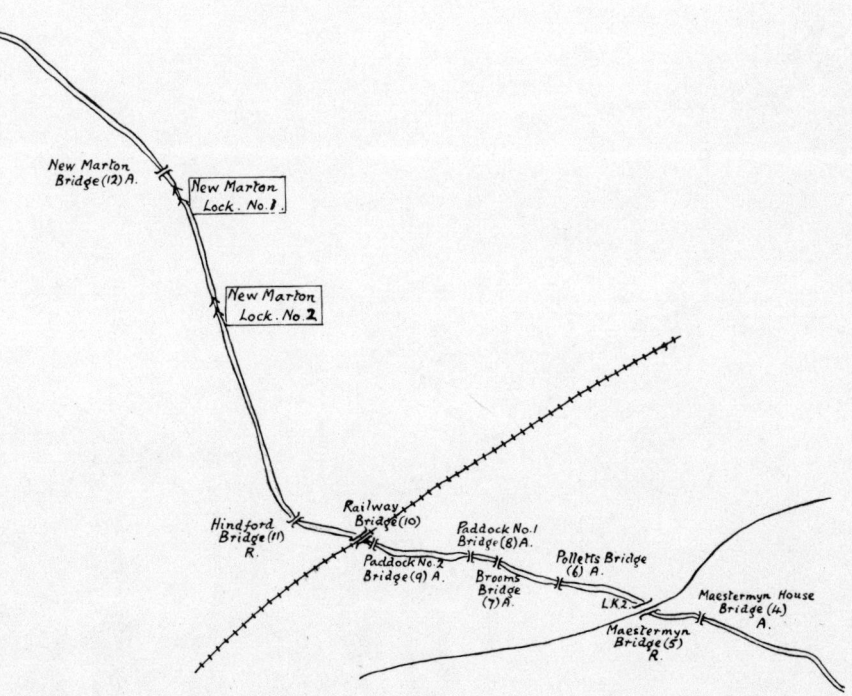

Ifton
Colliery

New Marton
Bridge (12) A.

New Marton
Lock. No. 1.

New Marton
Lock. No. 2

Hindford
Bridge (11)
R.

Railway
Bridge (10)

Paddock No. 2
Bridge (9) A.

Paddock No. 1
Bridge (8) A.

Brooms
Bridge
(7) A.

Polletts Bridge
(6) A.

L K 2.

Maestermyn House
Bridge (4)
A.

Maestermyn
Bridge (5)
R.

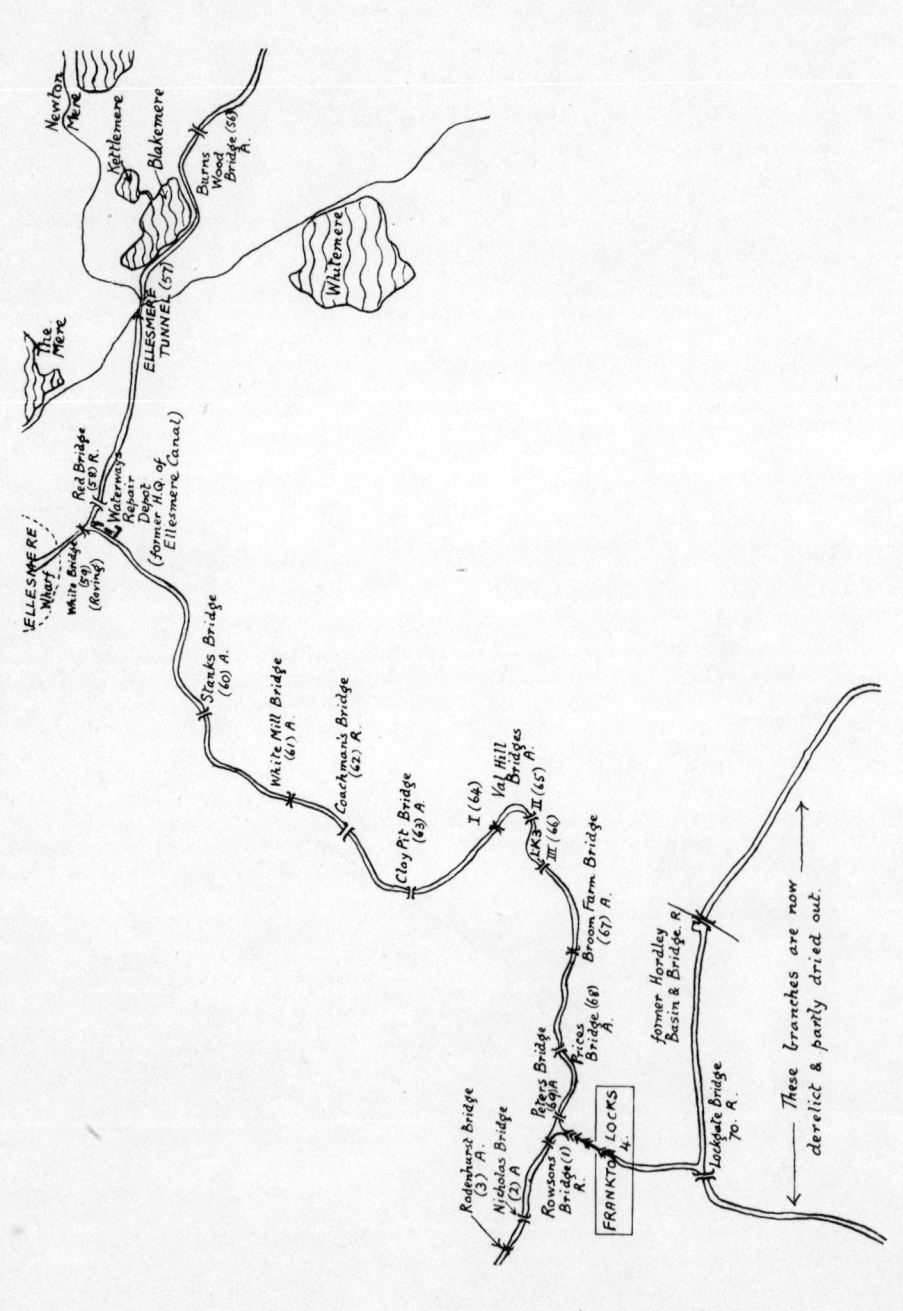

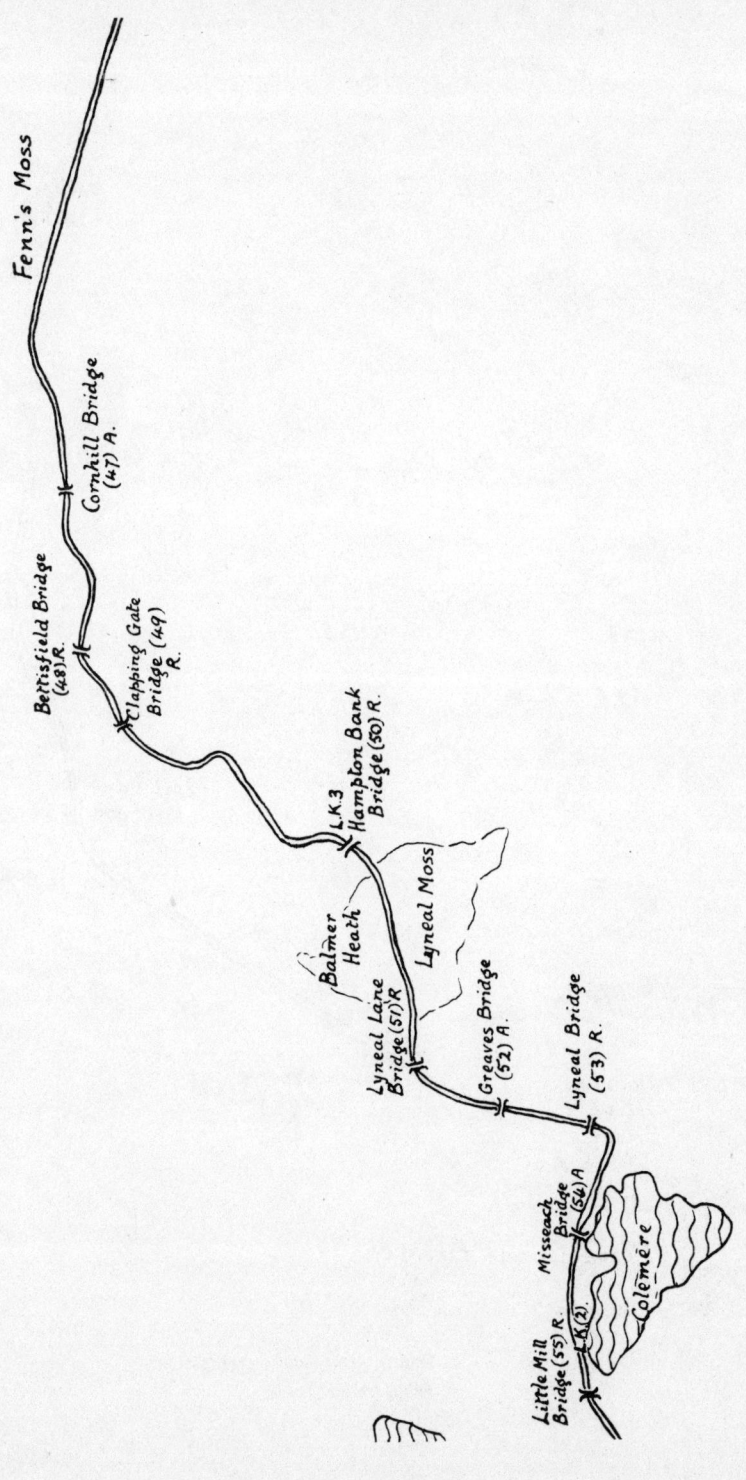

Fenn's Moss

Cornhill Bridge (47) A.

Bettisfield Bridge (48) R.

Clapping Gate Bridge (49) R.

L.K.3 Hampton Bank Bridge (50) R.

Lyneal Moss

Balmer Heath

Lyneal Lane Bridge (51) R.

Greaves Bridge (52) A.

Lyneal Bridge (53) R.

Misseach Bridge (54) A.

Colemere

Little Mill Bridge (55) R.

L.K.(2)

Springhill
Bridge
(41) A.

Tilstock Park
Lift-up Bridge
(42) R.

Platt Lane
Bridge
(43) R.

Whixall Moss

Morriss
Lift-up
Bridge
(45) A.

Roundthorn
Bridge (44) R.

Roving
Bridge (46)

← Prees Canal Branch

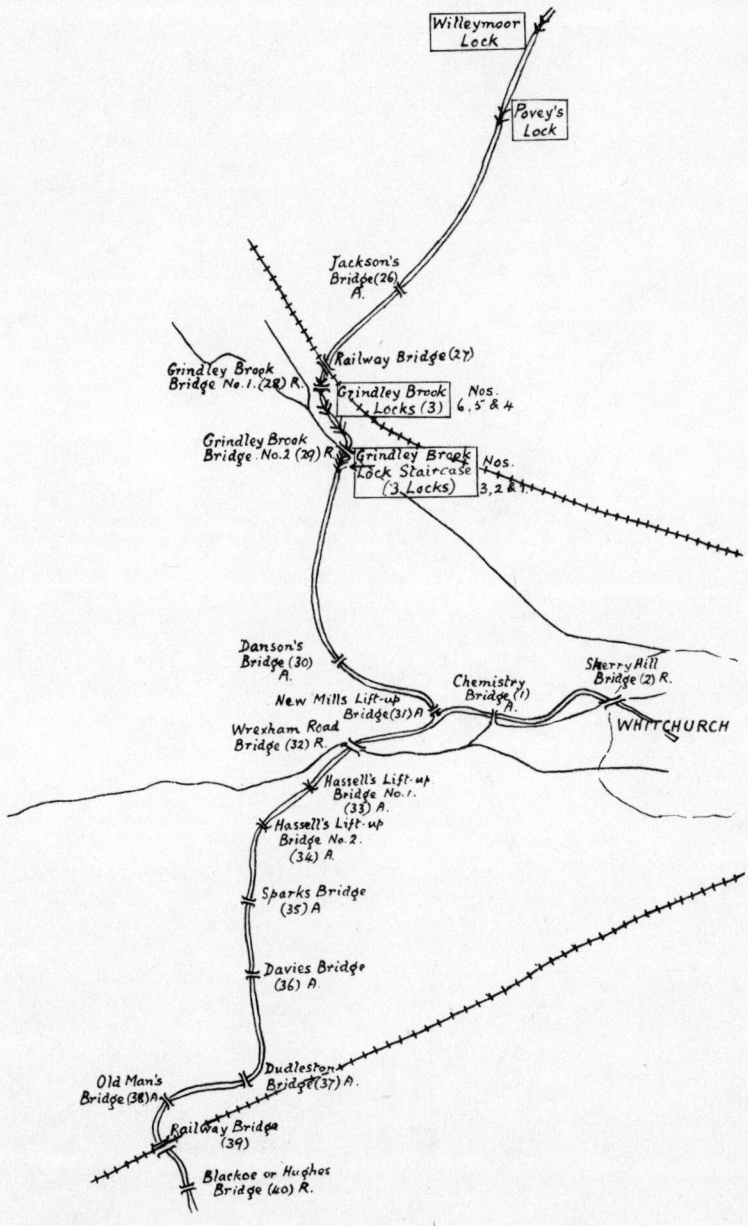

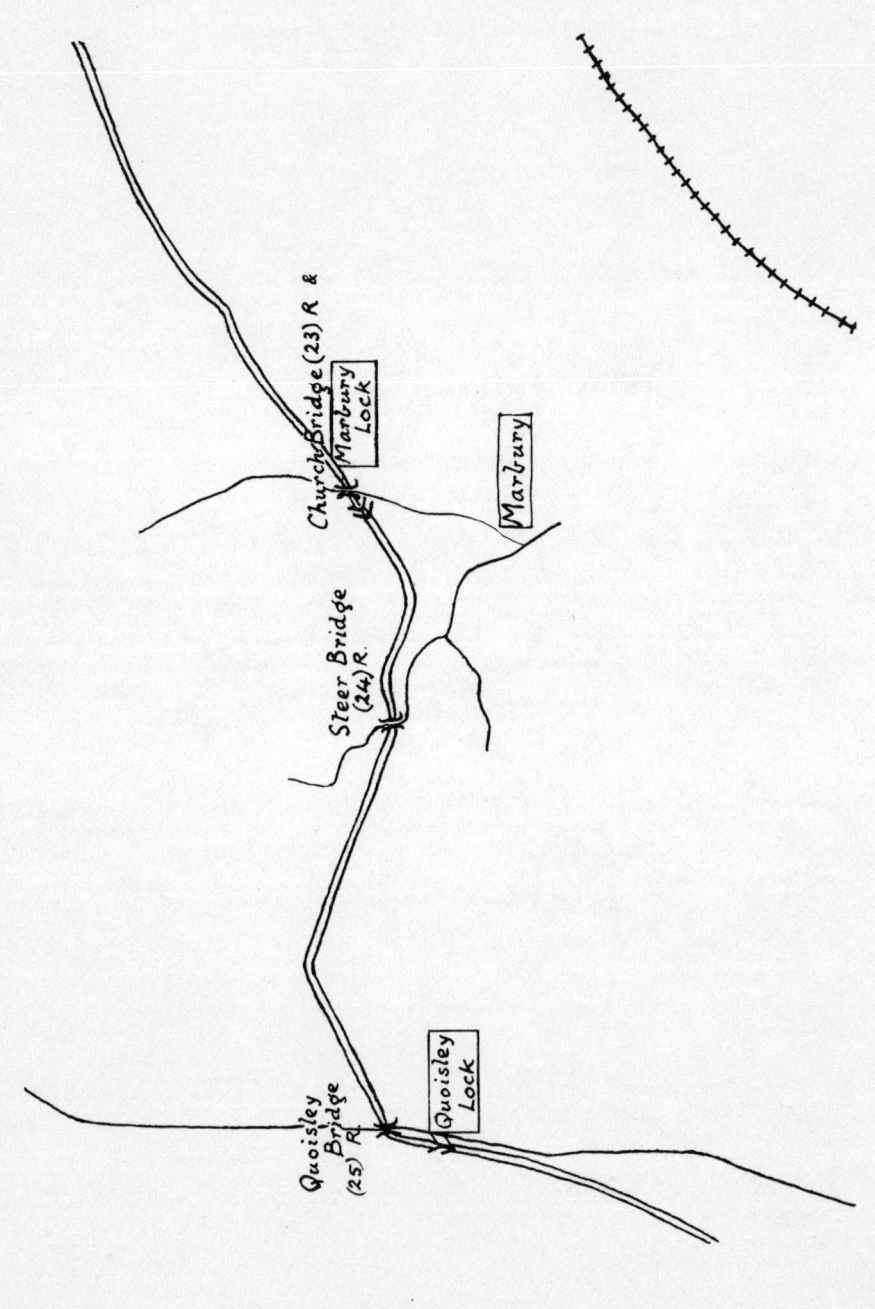

Church Bridge (23) R &

Marbury
Lock

Marbury

Steer Bridge
(24) R.

Quoisley
Lock

Quoisley
Bridge
(25) R

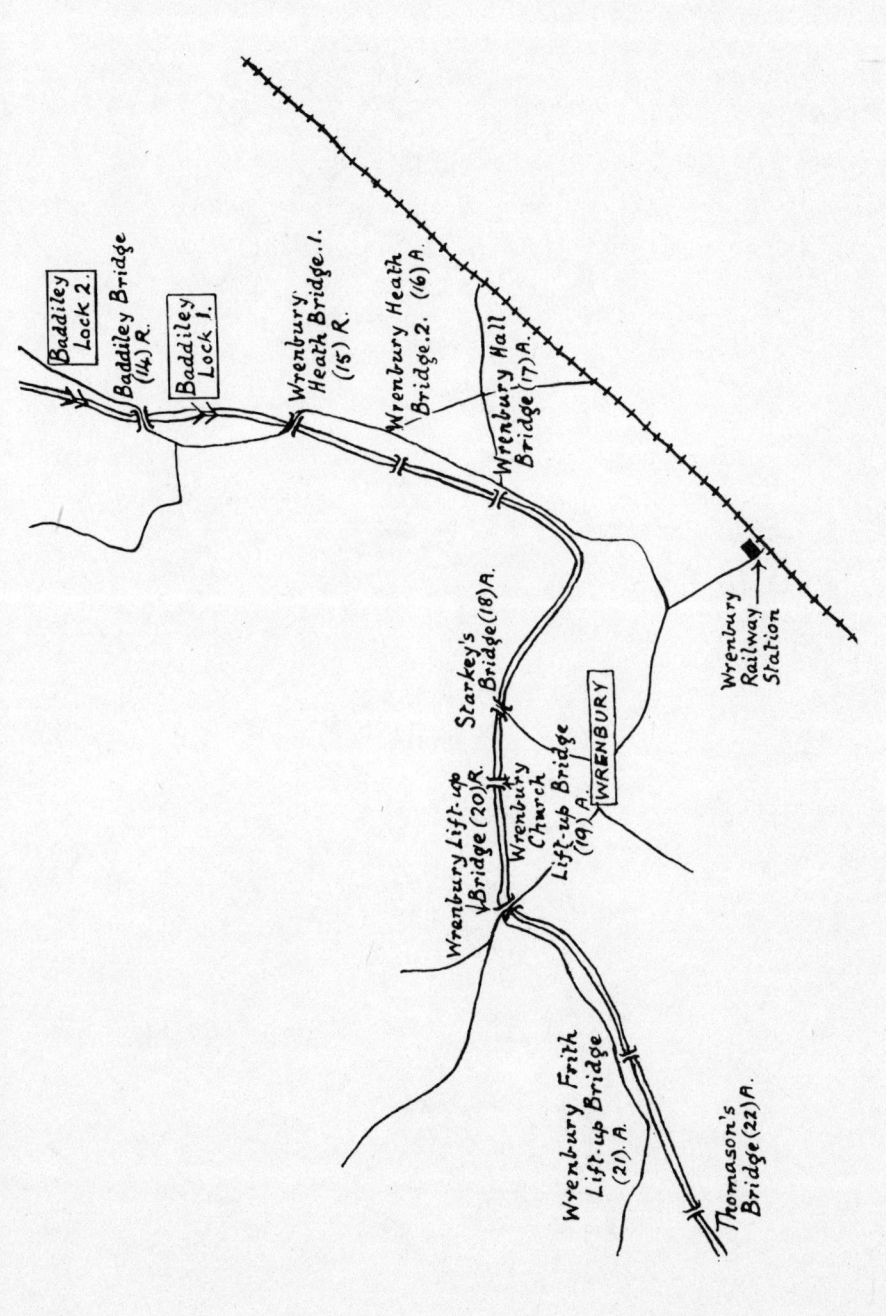

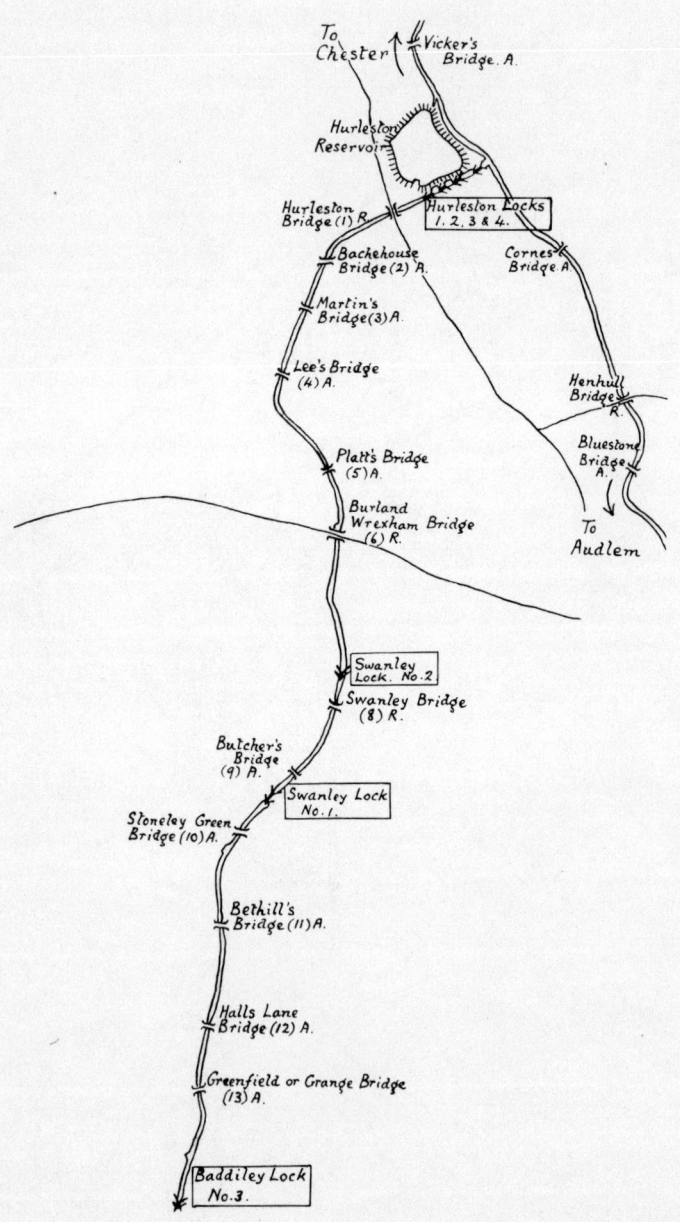

To Chester

Vicker's Bridge. A.

Hurleston Reservoir

Hurleston Bridge (1) R.

Hurleston Locks 1, 2, 3 & 4.

Cornes Bridge A

Backehouse Bridge (2) A.

Martin's Bridge (3) A.

Lee's Bridge (4) A.

Henhull Bridge R.

Platt's Bridge (5) A.

Bluestone Bridge A.

Burland Wrexham Bridge (6) R.

To Audlem

Swanley Lock. No.2

Swanley Bridge (8) R.

Butcher's Bridge (9) A.

Swanley Lock No.1.

Stoneley Green Bridge (10) A.

Bethill's Bridge (11) A.

Halls Lane Bridge (12) A.

Greenfield or Grange Bridge (13) A.

Baddiley Lock No.3.

adjoining pound to fill up the first lock there was so little water left in the pound that when we entered it we soon grounded and came to an abrupt halt. The lock-keeper solved the difficulty by letting water into the pound from the second lock; by repeating this procedure for each lock the *Beryl* climbed up through the remaining locks.

We were now in the old Ellesmere Canal with its beautifully clear water, but this desirable feature was accompanied by several undesirable ones. The canal was so shallow that almost every day we grounded at least once in spite of our shallow draft; there were many weeds which hindered our progress by getting twisted around our propeller - and not only weed - we picked up string, rope and even wire - and the wire-gauze filter soon became choked up with duckweed and frequently had to be cleaned out.

In spite of these minor troubles we made slow, steady progress, passing through a number of locks, some in picturesque rural surroundings. They were deserted and often so derelict that some of the lockgate paddle gear had broken away from the woodwork leaving them completely useless - at one lock there was only one paddle which would function, and the balance beam looked as if a hard push would have snapped it off.

The countryside was very peaceful. Sometimes trees lined the canal, sometime meadows. We still met the occasional heron or caught sight of a moorhen scuttling for safety amongst the reeds which sometimes grew so far out into the canal that only a narrow navigable channel was left; but our most frequent visitors were swans.

At 7.25 p.m. we met our first 'lift-up' bridge near Wrenbury. We passed two more before stopping for the night.

The next morning we continued our placid course through lovely rural surroundings with more swans racing ahead. We seemed to be moving through a deserted and forgotten world, where even the cows seemed to regard our passage with curiosity. There was no modernization here; no well kept towpath or clean cut edge to the canal. With its crumbling banks and wide fringes of reeds it was far more like a small river than a canal.

Soon, however, we entered a well-kept stretch, only to find the water level over a foot below normal, so that we grounded, and had to haul on the rope and use the punt pole, and work really hard. We were nearing Grindley Brook with its six locks, and the lock-keeper told us that the low water was due to the carelessness of a boat passing through during the night and leaving the paddles open. This had let so much water through from the upper level that he had no option but to close up everything until the level had built up again. By the time we arrived at the bottom lock there was barely enough water to float us. The first three locks were separated by short pounds, but they were followed by a 'staircase' of three locks, built as one unit.

When we had surmounted the 'staircase' we had worked through 25 locks and were not sorry to know that now we had a stretch of 21 miles to come before reaching the last two locks on the outward journey. Soon we reached the point where a short arm of the canal used to lead off to the Canal Basin at Whitchurch, but when we passed by there were only a few stagnant, weedy patches still left to be filled in; the lift-up bridge had lost its chain, so we had to use the boathook to open it.

The countryside now changed from undulating fields to parkland with grass and trees around Tilstock, and there was a further change after Platt Lane Bridge. Here we entered upon a straight stretch of canal almost a mile long with Roundthorn Bridge visible at its end, and with such a wide belt of reeds growing out from each bank that our boat brushed against them while navigating the narrow channel which was left.

Hedges hid our view along this stretch but after Roundthorn Bridge we could see far and wide over the desolate area of Whixall Moss, with its brown, peaty soil, small stacks of peat blocks, and stunted birch bushes everywhere. On these 'Mosses', where peat is still dug, there grow crossed-leaved heather, ling, bog rosemary, cranberry, iron grass, cotton grass and white-beaked sedge; snipe and curlew nest here; and one may find lizards and vipers. Today the peat is machine-cut, but it was still hand cut at the time of our cruise.

Soon we reached the point where the Prees branch left the main canal. Two-thirds of it was derelict, but contained enough water to make it a veritable water garden; the one-third was kept operational because clay was obtained from clay pits near it for repairing the canal banks. Just past the entrance to the Prees branch was a wide, straight stretch where the canal passed over Fenn's Moss; and we were making really good progress, when, without the slightest warning, the engine suddenly stopped dead! It was not long before we diagnosed the trouble - lack of petrol!

There was a garage at Bettisfield some two miles ahead, so we sent our boys on with an empty petrol can, while we pulled and punted the boat towards it. The boys returned empty handed as the garage had no petrol pump or spare petrol! After more hard work we finally reached Bettisfield Bridge where the proprietor of the *Nag's Head* offered to run me into the neighbouring village in his car, and I finally returned to the boat with two gallons of petrol. What a welcome sound the engine made as it started up once more! One gets attached to the steady beat of an engine, and any variation from the normal causes as much concern as if it were a living entity.

This unforseen delay had quite upset our timetable, as we had planned to spend the night in our house at Ellesmere. It was almost 7 p.m. as we started off once more and the sun was already going down, and as bridge after bridge was passed it became darker and darker. By the time we reached Miseach Bridge by Yell Wood at Colemere it was difficult to see anything clearly, and Blakemere which soon followed lived up to its old spelling 'Blackmere' as we skirted its edge and approached the darkened entrance to the Tunnel. It was so dark that the feeble light of two torches was not sufficient to show us the way through and we were brought to a sudden stop as our upperworks hit the arched roof. Fortunately the only damage was a broken glass jug.

Having hauled the *Beryl* through the rest of the Tunnel we carried on once more. Knowing these waters intimately was a great help in total darkness, but as we approached Red Bridge we were dazzled by the lights from a brightly lit pontoon boat *Magician* which was moored on the far side, and only just in time did we notice an unlit boat coming through the bridge-hole towards us. Finally, at 8.45 p.m. we tied up at the Ellesmere Wharf, and while two of us remained aboard, the other two members of the crew landed and went home for a hot bath and comfortable bed!

Before setting out once more we made sure we had enough petrol, as well as water and supplies of fresh food. We passed by Beech House, the H.Q. of the old Canal Company, and the Maintenance Depot where some 30 men were still employed. Soon we reached Welsh Frankton and passed by the northern end of the link with its four locks, and almost immediately passed by the *Duchess-Countess,* the famous packet boat which rested in a nearby field (see page 63).

Soon after mid-day we passed through the two New Marton Locks, the last two locks on our outward journey. It was extremely shallow here and we made very slow progress, grounding more than once. Crawling along slowly we passed our sister ship, the *Bobby,* at her moorings near St. Martin's Moor Bridge. This was a picturesque spot with a hump-backed bridge (now replaced by a modern road bridge), well made wharf, warehouse and bakery, with a background of trees. We tried bow-hauling and punting, but it was so shallow that when the punt pole got stuck it was quite easy to walk out into the canal to retrieve it.

At 5 o'clock we reached the *New Inn* at Gledrid, and the canal became more interesting. For a time it ran parallel to the main A5 road, following it round a curve. Then, while the road descended steeply to Chirk Bridge over the River Ceiriog, the canal had no option but to continue its level course along an embankment which became higher and higher in relation to the road until it assumed impressive proportions at Chirk Bank, and led on to the Chirk Aqueduct. There had been a break in this embankment in 1826 in very stormy weather; it gave way completely, damming the River Ceiriog below and diverting its waters so that within half an hour every pit belonging to the Chirk Bank Colliery was filled with water, earth and gravel, and so completely destroyed that they were never worked again. By a miracle this was the only night for several years that there were no men down the pit.

We crossed the Aqueduct at 5.30 p.m., two trains passing
by at a higher level on the neighbouring railway viaduct
before we reached the pool by the striking entrance to the
Chirk Tunnel. Being so long and dark we decided to pull our
boat through. The towpath was in fairly good condition, but
there were muddy patches, and a certain amount of water
dripped down from the arched roof and walls. In the distance
we could see the end of the perfectly straight tunnel. Then a
train passed over our heads in its separate tunnel with a distant
reverberating rumble; this, and the hollow sound of our
voices, produced a 'somewhat macabre effect, and it was quite
a relief to come out into the daylight once more.

The daylight was rather subdued, however, as the tunnel
was followed by a deep cutting nearly a mile long, the digging
of which 'was a tedious operation'. Earth must have been
washed down its steep sides during those early years, as three
years after its opening we read,

> During the dry weather in the Autumn the canal through the deep
> cutting at Chirk was cleaned out, and will now admit boats with
> full loading to pass.

Today the banks of the cutting are covered by a profuse
undergrowth of ferns, liverworts, mosses and brush-like
horsetails, growing amongst the many trees. Quite a number
of the trees had fallen down and their prostrate, moss-covered
trunks added to the illusion that we were travelling through
some damp, primaeval forest.

The railway ran parallel to the cutting, but at a higher
level, and was hidden from our view until we reached the end
of the cutting where it used to cross the inlet from the canal
by means of a bridge. Two years ago the canal inlet was filled
in and the underside of the railway bridge converted into an
embankment.

After passing through Whitehurst Tunnel we soon entered
the broad and beautiful valley of the River Dee, and our
attention was immediately focussed on the impressive railway
viaduct which crosses the valley at this point to Cefn Mawr.
Like the Chirk Railway Viaduct this was built by Henry
Robertson, the ceremony of keying the last arch being
performed by W. Ormsby Gore, M.P. on 25 August 1848.

With a length of 1,530 ft. and a height of 148 ft., with 19 arches, it was the largest viaduct in the country at that time. The tables at the gargantuan banquet which followed were loaded with such a quantity and variety of food and drink that a contemporary account reads like a page from the *Arabian Nights' Entertainment* - no less than 25 separate toasts were drunk. One can only wonder at the astonishing capacity of the human digestive system to withstand such an assault.

A short distance further on we sighted the main objective of our voyage, the slender-columned Pontcysyllte Aqueduct, but the dusk was deepening and our rate of travel was becoming slower and slower until we were virtually making no progress at all. The sound of the engine was quite normal, so we wondered if it might be something wrong with the transmission gear. By the time we reached the lift-up bridge just past the limekilns at Vroncysyllte we realized that it was useless to carry on, and so tied up for the night.

It was now 8 p.m. Across the valley the unlovely industrial town of Cefn Mawr sprawled over the hilly ground almost up to the far end of the Aqueduct where Monsanto Chemicals Ltd., literally covers every inch of the hill with its smoke stacks, factory buildings, furnaces, fractionating columns and waste heaps, in a confused and monstrous medley.

Dusk gave place to darkness, and the lights shone out. Gone was all the ugliness and squalor, and a marvellous transformation took place to a beautiful fairyland lit up by hundreds of tiny lights, the blue lights of the mercury vapour lamps outshining the yellow glow of the ordinary filament lamps. It was an unforgettable sight, and we came out from the cabin again and again, attracted to the scene almost as powerfully as moths are drawn to a lighted lantern. At last we had to retire, wondering what the morrow had in store for us.

The next morning, with much forboding, we made enquiries about local mechanics, but the replies were not very helpful. Although while doing the routine job of clearing obstructions from the propeller, we felt something rather elastic, and on giving a sudden pull out came a five foot length of cycle tyre

outer cover! The situation rapidly brightened and on starting
the engine at 7.8 a.m. everything went perfectly and we were
soon speeding along at four miles per hour. Almost
immediately we left the south side of the valley and turned
sharply northwards along the approach to the Pontcysyllte
Aqueduct where it runs along the top of the artificially
raised, tree covered embankment, over 1,000 ft. long, and
reaching a height of 75 ft. at the beginning of the Aqueduct.

Pontcysyllte was our Mecca, and as we entered it aboard
the *Beryl* we tried to visualise the scene on its first opening
on 26 November 1805, which followed so closely on Nelson's
great victory at Trafalgar. An eye-witness account of that
scene is given in Chapter 3. Now here we were 165 years
later. We admired the glorious scenery from our aerial stand-
point as we crossed over the River Dee, whose banks were
hidden by the foliage of innumerable trees. The shallow
water could be seen foaming over the shelving rocks, and
around the bases of the Aqueduct piers, although at this
height its sound was a mere murmur. The picturesque road
bridge and the several cottages scattered about the wooded
slopes of the valley might have been buildings in Lilliput.

It took us ten minutes to cross the Aqueduct, and then
while breakfast was being prepared by the cook the rest of
us landed and walked under the Aqueduct and down the
steep side of the river bank alongside the impressive pillars
which carried the iron arches supporting the cast iron trough.
A path through the trees and bushes brought us to river level
and we had a breath-taking view of the Aqueduct's slender
columns towering up high above the river and disappearing
from view on each side amongst the forest of trees which
covered the banks just here.

This 'wonder of the age' came quite early in Telford's
career; and although he went on to build the Menai and
Conway Suspension Bridges, the Gotha Canal across Sweden,
the Caledonian Canal across Scotland, a great many bridges
of stone and iron, as well as many roads and harbours, he
always kept a cherished place in his memory for the Pontcysyllte Aqueduct. It figures in the background of Telford's
portrait painted for the Institution of Civil Engineers, of
which he was the first President.

EARNINGS OF THE PACKET BOAT ON THE WIRRAL LINE

	1795	1796	1797	1798	1799	1800	1801
January		47 17 5½	45 3 8	56 0 6	38 14 4	63 18 0	77 13 3
February		44 18 9	46 9 7	50 0 4	32 8 5	70 12 7	84 4 10
March		53 13 5½	65 2 9	72 17 9	85 6 4	81 0 8	112 12 4
April		61 6 5	77 14 10	93 13 7	76 17 3	95 7 1	103 9 1
May		101 6 6	107 6 11	142 8 2	174 9 6	191 15 10	202 8 9
June		77 19 3	92 18 10	133 9 1	126 3 2	131 0 0	143 9 1
July	103 11 3	107 4 10	152 11 0	192 5 5	209 9 6	224 1 0	210 4 11
August	119 1 6	123 1 3	129 10 3	191 10 8	168 15 5	184 5 0	197 17 0
September	112 13 7	97 18 6	111 5 9	126 18 3	135 19 4	131 16 9	173 13 10
October	79 16 0	101 0 7	108 12 8	125 3 5	147 16 0	119 16 8	
November	42 19 0	44 5 9	54 14 2	67 5 6	68 8 2	69 16 9	
December	38 8 4	7 11 14	58 12 6	50 9 5	53 8 11½	75 6 2	
Totals £	496 9 8	868 4 1	1050 2 11	1302 2 1	1317 16 4½	1438 16 6	

Letter from Telford to John Knight (of Whitchurch)

Salop. 22 March, 1802

Dear Sir,

I have here enclosed you a statement of the Canal Packet up to Oct. 1801, when it was let at a rent annually.

I am yours sincerely,

Thos Telford.

APPENDIX 2

TONNAGE RETURNS

Tonnage from 25th December, 1807 to 24th June, 1808

SHROPSHIRE LINE

	£	s.	d.	£	s.	d.	£	s.	d.
Limestone into Montgomeryshire	185	15	11						
Lime Coal into Montgomeryshire	725	7	9						
Limestone into Salop.	657	6	11						
Lime Coal into Salop.	558	3	4						
Burnt Lime	279	16	3						
				2408	10	2			
Fire Coal from Pontcysylte Aqueduct into Montgomeryshire	512	8	0						
Fire Coal from Pontcysylte Aqueduct to Whitchurch and Ellesmere	671	17	9						
Fire Coal from Pontcysylte Aqueduct to Weston	19	1	6						
From Chester to Whitchurch	2	18	6						
From Chester to Wrenbury	10	6	10						
				1216	12	7			
Timber out of Shropshire to Chester	329	9	9						
Timber out of Montgomeryshire to Chester	154	2	9						
				483	12	6			
Commercial Goods				399	6	7			
Grain and Malt				625	14	6			
Building Stone				46	13	9			
Slates				141	19	10			
Bark				167	1	2			
Deal and Timber form Liverpool and Chester				48	10	3			
Brick, Lead, Iron, Wool, Grinding Stones, etc.				150	8	0			
Railway				102	2	11			
							5783	12	3
Rents on above lines							81	11	0
Graving docks							8	11	0
Weighing and Indexing Boats							215	0	0
Tonnage on Wirral Line	1196	16	4						
Rents on Wirral Line	726	18	11						
Graving Docks on Wirral Line	2	8	0						
							1962	3	3
							£8050	17	6

APPENDIX 3

ABSTRACT OF TONNAGE (mainly 1809)

	25 Dec. 1808 - 25 Mar. 1809			25 Mar. 1809 - 24 June 1809			24 June 1809 - 29 Sep. 1809		
	£	s.	d.	£	s.	d.	£	s.	d.
SHROPSHIRE LINES:									
Limestone boated into Montgomeryshire	41	10	5	80	0	0	64	4	5
Lime Coals boated into Montgomeryshire	91	3	2	556	17	1	239	9	6
Limestone boated into Shropshire	206	10	6	447	3	8	328	3	0
Lime Coals boated into Shropshire	197	10	3	262	8	11	291	16	7
Burnt Lime	15	13	8	282	13	9	304	4	4
	552	8	0	1631	7	11	1227	17	10
Fire Coals from over Pontcysylte Aqueduct into Montgomeryshire	218	8	10	291	9	10	383	18	1
Fire Coals from over Pontcysylte Aqueduct into Whitchurch and Ellesmere	274	9	10	337	3	9	416	11	6
Fire Coals from over Pontcysylte Aqueduct into Weston	11	7	4	7	10	9	8	7	1
From Chester to Whitchurch and Wrenbury	11	3	7	44	19	1	11	4	8
	515	9	7	681	3	5	820	1	4
Timber out of Shropshire to Chester	112	7	3	150	9	8	156	7	5
Timber out of Montgomeryshire to Chester	98	14	10	82	13	11	154	9	11
	211	2	1	233	3	7	310	17	4
Commercial Goods	211	2	1	174	16	0	237	8	7
Grain and Malt	253	10	0	143	16	0	155	18	1
Building Stone	15	1	5	27	0	10	18	11	0
Slates	16	4	6	120	18	9	156	3	5
Bark	20	5	5	113	11	9	265	11	6
Iron	1	2	1	7	2	2	6	11	0
Deal Timber from Liverpool and Chester	2	13	0	11	12	5	2	4	5
Bricks, Freestone, Lead, Wool, etc.	65	4	9	128	19	9	130	12	5
Railway	35	17	1	68	16	0	64	0	0
Totals of above	1900	0	0	3342	8	7	3395	16	11
Rents on the above lines	38	7	0	29	17	6	29	7	0
Graving docks on the above lines	4	4	0	4	15	0	6	6	0
Weighing and Indexing Boats	22	10	0	31	10	6	1	3	0
Shropshire Line—Grand Totals	1965	1	0	3408	11	7	3432	12	11
WIRRAL LINE:									
Tonnage on Wirral Line	502	12	0	531	17	8	679	19	9
Rents	368	3	9	368	4	11	368	4	11
Graving dock rents	7	8	0	2	6	0	8	4	0
Uses of Cranes	15	5	0	12	15	0	12	5	0
Wirral and Shropshire Lines—Combined Totals	2868	9	9	4323	15	2	4501	6	7

SELECT BIBLIOGRAPHY

Books:

Thomas Telford, *Life of Thomas Telford* (ed. by Rickman), (1838).

Annual Register, *Opening of Pontcysyllte Aqueduct*, 26 November 1805.

'T.C.L.' (The Ffrwd Canal), *Brymbo Works Magazine*, Vol. 2, No. 6 (September 1923).

S. Lewis, *Topographical Dictionary of Wales* (1833).

G. G. Lerry, *Collieries of Denbighshire*.

Prof. Dodd, *North Wales Coal Industry*.

Samuel Bagshaw, *Shropshire* (1851).

MacDermot, *History of the Great Western Railway*.

Geology of the country around Wrexham—Part II. Coal measures and newer formations (1928).

Geological Memoirs, 138. *Geology of the country around Wem.*

J. Plymley, *General View of the Agriculture of Shropshire.*

S. Smiles, *Lives of Engineers—Telford.*

G. G. Lerry, *Henry Robertson* (1949).

D. L. Davies, *The Glyn Valley Tramway* (1962).

The Journal of Transport History, Vol. III, No. 1 (May 1957).

C. A. Hadfield, *Canals of the West Midlands* (1966).

L. T. C. Rolt, *Thomas Telford* (1958).

L. T. C. Rolt, *The Inland Waterways of England* (1950).

L. T. C. Rolt, *Narrow Boat* (1948).

Newspapers and Magazines:

Shrewsbury Chronicle (1794-6).

Oswestry Advertiser (1860).

C. A. Hadfield, 'Telford, Jessop and Pontcysyllte' in *Journal of Railway and Canal Historical Society*, Vol. xv, No. 4 (October 1969).

J. Horsley Denton, 'By rail and canal to Mid-Wales in 1853', *Journal of the Railway and Canal Historical Society*, Vol. xvi, No. 2 (April 1970).

Parliamentary Acts for the Ellesmere Canal (1772, 1777, 1778, 1793, 1796, 1801, 1802, 1804, 1810, 1813, 1827, 1830).

Minutes of Evidence before the Committee on the British Transport Commission Bill (House of Commons session, 1953-4). Canal.

Reports to the Ellesmere Canal Committee:
Report to the General Assembly of the Ellesmere Canal Proprietors (November 1805).
Reports to the Committee for: 23 September 1793; 4 December 1794; 5 January 1795; 8 July 1795; 10 August 1795; 28 October 1795; 27 November 1795; 25 November 1801; 30 June 1802; 28 November 1804; 27 August 1821; 29 July 1824; 30 July 1835.

Reports from Jessop:
14 July 1795; 5 February 1800; 8 December 1795.

Reports from Telford:
21 October 1795; 13 December 1800.

Statements:
23 September 1801 (Minutes); 25 November 1801 (J. Knight); 12 April 1809 (issued by Committee to the public).

Letters:
Joseph Turner (17 November 1801).
Thomas Telford (30 November 1801).
Earl of Bridgewater (3 March 1802; 11 September 1809).

Tonnage Returns:
(24 June—September 1808.)

Estate Papers:

Bridgewater Estate papers.
Sweeney Hall Estate papers.

Maps:

Joseph Turner, Thomas Morris, William Cowley and John Chamberlain, *Plan for the Eastern Canal* (1792). Shropshire County Archives.

Several early maps, most of them unsigned and undated. Shropshire County Archives.

Plan for the Western Canal. Cheshire County Archives.

Ordnance Survey maps, 1873 (scale 1:25,000).

G. R. Jebb, *Map of Ellesmere Port* (1882).

S.U.R. & C. Company, *Map of proposed scheme for converting the Ellesmere Canal into a railway* (1845).

G.W.R. Railway Plans for railways in the vicinity of Oswestry, Rednal, Ellesmere, Whitchurch and Wrexham. (1859-1864.)

Minutes of the Ellesmere Canal Company.

ACKNOWLEDGEMENTS

H. W. Mackey, *Duchess-Countess.*

The late Frank Peate, *Maesbury Corn Mill.*

Employees at the Ellesmere Canal Maintenance Depot, especially Mr. Hughes and Mr. Moody. Shown much of the canal maintenance work.

Manchester Ship Canal Office, Ellesmere Port. *Port Installations.*

Librarian of the Ellesmere Port Public Library.

Librarian of the Shrewsbury Public Library.

Mr. King, *Wilson King Flour Mills, Liverpool.*

Charles Hadfield, *Ellesmere Canal, and canal matters in general.*

D. L. Davies, *Glyn Valley Tramway.*

INDEX